Craft and Art – The Business

Also available from Elliot Right Way Books:

The Right Way to Start Your Own Business
Book-keeping Properly Explained
Upholstery Properly Explained
Improve Your Piano Playing
Escape From the Rat Race

Craft and Art The Business

by

Elizabeth White

Typeset in 11½/14 pt Legacy Serif Book by Letterpart Ltd., Reigate, Surrey.

Printed and bound in Great Britain by Guernsey Press Co. Ltd., Guernsey, Channel Islands.

The *Right Way Plus* series is published by Elliot Right Way Books, Brighton Road, Lower Kingswood, Tadworth, Surrey, KT20 6TD, U.K. For information about our company and the other books we publish, visit our website at www.right-way.co.uk

Contents

Dedication

For Katherine

Acknowledgements

Many people have supported, encouraged and helped me with the preparation of this book. I would particularly like to thank the following: Liz Barclay, Janet Barnes (Director, The Craft Council), Angie and Paul Boyer (*The Craftsman*), Sally Bulgin (*The Artist*), Frank Dawes (Bolton Institute), Jennifer Hallam (Yorkshire Arts), Barney Hare Duke (Northwest Arts), Tom Walker (Small Business Service), colleagues at Manchester Business Consortium and Anne Kennedy, Crafts Council of Ireland. And a special thank you to all the craftworkers and artists whose problems prompted me to write this book.

Introduction

Could you use your skills to produce an income?

Do you want employment that uses your creative abilities, which you find fulfilling and where you can retain some control over your working environment? If the answer is 'yes', and you have the necessary skills, then this book is for you. This book was written to help you start an art, craft or design business which is successful, enjoyable and profitable.

Do you have the right attitude to make it work?

Are you an independent person, not afraid to go in one direction while others go in another?

Being an entrepreneur involves taking risks, selectively ignoring the well-meaning advice of others and learning to trust your instincts. You need to be able to cope with the absence of a regular salary payment. Finding a gap in the market and being prepared to offer the customer something different is vital.

Do you believe in yourself, are you a positive person?

If you don't believe in yourself no-one else will either. It's not easy to be positive when things go wrong but it is essential if you're to succeed. Every business has its highs and lows and the ability to keep trying when the going gets tough is very important.

Do you know how to set goals, and have you the persistence to achieve them?

A good business plan is vital for any business, and goal-setting is a skill which you can learn. Writing a business plan is not complicated but it is important.

Are you well-organised?

Keeping books, sending invoices and so on is an essential part of running a business. Set up the administration systems before you start. Find a system that suits you and keep everything up-to-date.

Do you have the essential creative skills to make the product?

If your skills are not developed sufficiently to produce goods suitable for selling, then go for training to improve them or to learn new skills. Training in art and craft skills is available either full- or part-time in most regions. If yours is an unusual skill you might be able to learn by working alongside an expert. There are all sorts of opportunities available: make the most of them to increase your competitiveness.

Do you find it easy to ask for help?

Craftworkers and artists are friendly and supportive to colleagues, so help is always available but you need to ask.

You will also need to ask professionals, such as accountants, bank managers and solicitors, for their advice. Being afraid to take professional advice when it is needed is a false economy.

Do you have regular contact with other self-employed people?

Creating a support network of other people in a similar situation is very valuable and can help you during the low times. Guilds, artists' groups and craftworkers' associations are an excellent way of learning about the industry.

Are you a good money manager?

No matter how brilliant your product, if you cannot control the money then you will not survive long in business. If your financial skills are poor you will need to improve on them or find someone to help. A simple book-keeping system is essential, either using an account book or computer if preferred. Always send invoices and statements on time and pursue unpaid bills.

Are you flexible and adaptable?

Many craftworkers start out in one business and end up in another. You need to watch for opportunities and changing markets. Craftworkers must be able to adapt to fashions in the marketplace; new materials are always coming on the market so you must constantly be looking for ways to improve your business.

Do you have energy, drive and patience?

A new business may not begin to make a profit for a number of years. You may need to supplement your income by working part-time during the start-up period and you will almost certainly have to work more than the normal 40 hours. You will also need the support and involvement of your loved ones!

Sounds like a lot of hard work? So why do it? Because making a living from your own skills is most rewarding. Having customers who want to buy products that you have designed or made will give you incredible satisfaction. The world of creative people is stimulating and exciting, and you will make new friends by attending fairs, joining guilds and taking part in exhibitions. Running a creative business is likely to take over your life but I guarantee you will never have had so much fun!

Turning the dream of having your own craft based business into reality is not always easy but, with the help of this book, you really can make it work! The best way to use this book is to read it all the way through initially and then to use it as a reference for particular problems.

Convinced? Then follow the advice in this book and change your life!

Chapter 1:

You Can Sell Your Work!

Freedom, flexibility and an enjoyable lifestyle are the main reasons people give for choosing to start a craft-based business. The ability to decide where you live and work is also an important factor in selecting a way of life that creates few millionaires but a lot of satisfied people.

Few craftworkers create with the intention of selling their work; the joy of creating and producing work that pleases them is reward enough. For some people this situation never changes; for others there comes a time when they want to reach a wider audience, and begin exhibiting and offering their work for sale. Although it can be difficult to part with work that one has created, it is undeniably a special feeling when someone, particularly a complete stranger, is prepared to part with his hard-earned cash to buy your work.

Starting out

Starting a business is like taking a journey: you have a better chance of reaching your destination if you know where you want to go. In the same way as you plan a journey, you need to work out exactly what it is you want to achieve before you start your business. Everyone needs a plan and it should be written down – not on the back of an envelope, but properly so you can keep track of where you are going. Plans are not set in stone, and on any journey you can always take a detour, but if you don't know your destination then you've got little chance of reaching it.

First of all you need to decide what you want to achieve in your business and set yourself some goals.

Your short-term goals could be:

1. To exhibit your work at a craft fair.
2. To enter your paintings in at least six exhibitions.
3. To join a local craft guild and exhibit with them.
4. To find four shops to sell your handmade cards.
5. To work out the cost and find market opportunities for turning your paintings into prints.

Your long-term goals could be:

1. To achieve a turnover of £XX,000 per year in the first year.
2. To have your work on display in twenty galleries.
3. To export your work.

Decide where you want to go and then work out how you are going to get there, step by step. Each chapter of this book gives you help and information on one aspect of the business. Before we look at the details, let's take a look at some of the considerations involved in starting and running a craft business.

Finding your niche

You may already have a particular skill and know exactly what you want to make, so if there is a market for this product then you are in business! If there is little demand for this type of work you may need to learn a new skill or adapt your skills to suit the marketplace. Alternatively, you may be able to *create* a market for your products; they may be so original that no one has thought of them before. However, building a market from scratch is a time-consuming and expensive process and, without the resources of a large organisation, virtually impossible to achieve. Finding a space in the marketplace and filling it is certainly the more sensible option!

The cornerstone of a creative business is the ability to produce goods that are both saleable and have a high level of quality and artistic design. Being successful involves making something suitable for the marketplace, and at the same time being comfortable with what you produce. Craftworkers and artists are creative people and the chance to express their creativity is the main reason they choose to work in this field. For them, success in terms of earning a living depends on finding the right balance between making what they like and what will sell.

Before you start marketing your work, you should be able to answer yes to the following:

- Is your work of sufficient quality for people to purchase it?
- Are you working in a style that people want?
- Do you have enough work ready to sell?
- Are you able to produce enough pieces for potential buyers?

Understanding profit

One of the aims of this book is to help creative people increase their sales and profits to a level at which they can make a living. Some of you will be struggling to earn enough money to make the business work, other people know what they should do and choose not to do it. For some people the 'profit' in the business stands for an improved and more enjoyable lifestyle. 'Profit' can also be measured in increased knowledge and skills so, if you have a difficult year financially, look at what you've learnt. *You* are your business and any investment in you is the same as investment in plant and machinery for a different type of business.

Pricing your work

Most craftworkers do not spend enough time pricing their work. You should cost out every item you make. People who have been in business a long time think they can guess but you may be surprised how much it is actually costing you to produce something. Some materials, such as paint and clay, are not taken into account, which can lead artists and craftworkers to fall into the trap of selling at a loss. Whilst it is very difficult to price fine art or sculpture as the reputation of the artist plays such an important role, it is relatively easy to cost something like ceramics. Often, potters will look at the amount of clay used as the only cost involved and sell a jug for £5. When the price is worked out correctly, and overheads and time taken into consideration, the correct cost may be £10, which means that every time the potter sells a jug he is giving away £5. Would you stand on a street corner and give away £5 notes? Of course not. So you cannot afford to under-price your work. If you have been in business a while and are not making a profit then turn to page 94 and use the formulas given to calculate prices for your work.

Funding

Deciding on the area in which you want to work will also be limited by the finance available. Setting up costs for some crafts, such as that of the silversmith, are expensive; those for others, like, for example, silkscreen printing are relatively cheap. It may be inexpensive to rent a large studio at the top of an old mill, but getting your finished work out to galleries and into exhibitions could be time-consuming and expensive.

You may be lucky enough to find funding from the Crafts Council, your local Arts Council or the Prince's Trust, or you may be in an area which offers start-up grants. Funding from these sources will generally only help with start-up costs and you will need to fulfil certain criteria. Unless you have a lot of finance available you will probably need to start earning straight away. You could follow the path of many craftworkers and work part-time to finance a period in which you put together your business plan and design your product range.

Running a business

If this is your first venture in running a business you will need to develop business skills in order to achieve your objectives. Selling your work is not easy; you need to learn about marketing, pricing, how to identify opportunities and acquire all the other skills needed to run a small business. Makers often suffer under the illusion that, if they are good enough, people will seek them out – they fail to realise that paintings and craftwork need to be sold in the same way as other goods. In other words, people need to be able to find them in order to buy them. Try and identify which skills you need. If you really are hopeless with money then go on a course or find someone to do your books. Don't neglect your administration. The systems that are suggested in Chapter 6 are simple but need to be kept up-to-date to make them effective.

Promoting yourself

To further your career as an artist it is essential that you develop the art of self-promotion. The more time and effort you spend on promoting yourself, the better your chances of success. People like to meet artists and craftworkers to talk to them about their work, so be prepared to do this. You need to remember that many collectors like to know something about the maker and, if possible, meet them. Be prepared to attend your own exhibitions and show people round your studio. You also need to network amongst fellow artists, join your local art club, go to exhibitions, and perhaps become a friend of your local art gallery. Most exhibitions are the result of personal contact, so get out and about and make contacts. There is more about self-promotion in Chapter 10.

The right attitude

To have the right attitude you have to believe in your work and to make a positive commitment to its worth. You have to believe that people not only need but also want your work and you can provide for this by doing something you love.

Commitment

You need a commitment not only to producing the work but to selling it as well. Before you can approach a gallery for an exhibition you need a substantial body of work. For a stand at a craft fair you will need a range of products. To produce this you will need a certain level of discipline, particularly if you also have to do other work to pay the bills in the meantime.

The marketplace

Before you start to sell your work you need to identify your customer, to decide who is the person most likely to buy your work. When you know who your customers are then you can identify where they buy from and try and have your work on display in these places. For instance, if you specialise in garden ceramics, the local garden centre may be a better place to sell your work than a gallery. An expensive range of handmade cards would sell better in an upmarket gift shop than a market stall.

Art and craftwork make luxury purchases and as such are in competition with many other goods. Your work will need to be innovative, attractive and of good quality to be successful in obtaining its place in the marketplace. Individuals rather than organisations usually purchase craftwork and people are more selective when spending their own money, which means that they will look for added value. Artists and craftworkers have a natural advantage in this area, as their products are unique.

Why do people buy art and craftwork?

People buy individually created products because they like something different; a piece of jewellery that is unique, a vase that is not in every shop on the high street or an original work of art. Customers also enjoy actually meeting the person who makes the goods and this can be a bonus for artists and craftworkers who sell their products themselves, either at their workshop or studio or through craft fairs and exhibitions.

Some skills will never be viable as a business as the cost of the labour involved makes the goods unprofitable. Lace making is one example of a craft for which it is difficult to obtain a realistic price: a garment may take one thousand hours to make and yet have a market value of £600. If this applies to your chosen craft you may need to teach the craft in order to supplement your income.

Competing with mass produced goods

Working in an age of mass production has advantages and disadvantages. People have become used to cheap products but, at the same time, many people are looking for something different and this is the area in which the individual maker can succeed.

In order to create a successful business you will need to:

- Make something that appeals to a small group of people rather than trying to cater for a mass market.
- Always include as part of your work something that requires your specific skills.
- Develop a style that is unique to you. You may eventually have help with the more mundane production areas but there should always be an element that is yours and yours alone.
- Promote the fact that your products are unique and that they have been created rather than produced.
- Seek out unusual materials, ones that cannot be used with mass production techniques.

- Research your market carefully and find out exactly where the gap is. Finding the right niche can make all the difference between failure and success.

The craft community

On becoming a craftworker you will join one of the most exciting and interesting business communities. Craftworkers are very supportive; they help each other in a way that is unusual amongst competitors in other industries. Networking with other craftworkers is important, particularly if you are working from home or by yourself. Attending craft shows will keep you in touch, or you could try joining a guild. Becoming a craftworker is a way of life and, be warned, it is highly addictive!

The art community

The art community is equally supportive and friendly but it does tend to be less well organised if not a little chaotic. Taking space in an established studio is a good way to make contacts and find out what is going on. Attend exhibitions and gallery openings to increase your network. Art school graduates may find that life drawing classes at colleges or studios provide good networking opportunities. Older artists may find joining a local art society to be more useful.

Chapter 2:

Business Planning

Starting your own business

Earning part or all of your income as an artist means that you are running a small business. At first this can seem to be a daunting prospect. Unless you have experience in the business sector you may not be familiar with producing invoices, negotiating contracts and pricing work so that you make a profit, but these are all part of the world of business. All the aspects of the business have to blend together. You have to produce enough work to satisfy customers and the finance needs to be there at the right time to pay the bills. Keeping records is also very important in a business, as is knowing the facts about tax, National Insurance and self-assessment.

There are different structures for running your own business. Each has its advantages and disadvantages. To understand its respective merits and drawbacks, and the procedures demanded in accounting for tax, seek professional advice and talk to those who have already trodden that particular path. The types are listed below.

Sole trader

This is the simplest method of trading and is the one that most craftworkers choose. You control your business;

you make the decisions and decide your own future. You will be liable to pay income tax and class 4 National Insurance on your profits.

Partnership

A partnership is legally defined as two or more people in business together with a view to making a profit. It is always advisable to have the terms of the partnership in the form of a written and signed partnership agreement. The Partnership Act of 1890 governs the partnership if there is no formal agreement. Even when partnerships involve members of the same family it is important that you take professional advice and draw up an agreement.

A limited company

A limited company is a separate entity from its members. The company owns the business, not you. The main advantage of this method of trading is that if the business were to fail, you and your personal assets would be protected. You will be an employee of the company and receive a salary, and/or dividends if you are a shareholder. Regulations governing limited companies are complicated, so if you are thinking of going into business as a limited company you need all the more to get advice from an accountant or a solicitor as to whether it will be suitable for you. Should you choose to sign a personal guarantee over a loan from your bank etc., or allow them to have a charge on property you own separately from the business, beware! Those assets would *not* then be protected by the limited company status.

Having decided on your method of trading, you can always change from one format to another. You should, however, be aware that, although it is relatively easy for a sole trader to take on a partner or for a partnership to be dissolved, it is more difficult to liquidate a limited company and transfer this to an individual or partnership.

The business plan

A properly thought-out business plan is the basis of a successful business. You wouldn't dream of starting out on an unfamiliar journey without a map and you shouldn't even consider going into business without a business plan. Creative people often think that a business plan will restrict them and stifle their creativity. In fact, just the opposite is true. It is much easier to change direction and take advantage of opportunities if you know as much as possible about your business and its objectives.

One mistake that people make is to think of a business plan in purely financial terms. In fact, it should consider all aspects of a business. A good business plan will consist of seven main areas of work. These are: the business; the product; marketing; operational details; finance; management and the future.

The business

This section should include information on the type of business yours is to be, whether it is a sole trader, partnership, or a limited company. Detail the background to the business: are you taking over an existing workshop or leasing a property? Identify the goals you want to achieve, and give a general overview of your aims and objectives. Don't forget to say why there is a need for this type of business and why you will succeed.

The product

In this section you need to specify details of the type of product you are going to produce and the range of products you intend to market. This should include the innovation and design element and how you intend to maximise this. Most importantly, you need to specify your Unique Selling Proposition, the factor that is going to guarantee your product a place in the market.

Marketing

This section will be concerned with how you will introduce your product to your customers. A proper marketing strategy is important if you want your business to provide you with a living. You need to identify exactly who your customers are and then work out how you are going to reach them and persuade them to buy your goods. This section should also include details of how you will operate your pricing structure and include a strategy for advertising and public relations.

Operational details

Operating a craft as a hobby is very different from running a business. All the aspects of the business have to blend together. The production levels need to match the number of sales, the finance available needs to be there at the right time and you need to have people available when needed. Keeping records is very important to a business and it is vital in the first year. This section also needs to include details of manufacturing facilities - their location, equipment and suppliers.

Finance

All money matters should be highlighted in this section and a proper cash flow produced. Capital requirements and a forecast balance sheet for one year should be included. You will also need to give details of the finance available. The cash flow is particularly important, as this will allow you to measure the results against the projected figures and use the differences to adapt the plan and change priorities if necessary.

Management

The main person in the business will obviously be you, and possibly your partner. At this stage you probably do not intend to employ anyone else, but you still need to consider the possibility of what you will do when the business expands or grows. You should give details of any business training that you have undertaken to enable you to run a business and the systems you intend to use. There are basically two types of management: planned and reactive. The majority of craftworkers, in fact the majority of small businesses, use the reactive method. Without exception they could all improve their profitability if they used the planned method. Good management means making sure that all the parts of the plan work together, and this is as important as your ability to create if you are running a craft business.

The future

Although you may find it difficult to think beyond the next twelve months, when running a business you really need to consider your short- and long-term objectives. If you are starting off at craft fairs, perhaps you intend to open your own studio one day? Or might your long-term plan be to export? What sort of finance will you need long term? A well thought-out future plan could give a prospective lender confidence that you intend to work at this business and really make a go of it.

The length of the plan

Unless you are trying to raise a considerable amount of finance then the plan will only need to be about two or three pages long. The plan should be supported by other documents, such as a CV detailing your career to date, exhibitions and commissions as well as credit references and testimonials from suppliers, employers or customers.

Uses for the plan

Even if you don't need to borrow money and are financing everything yourself you still need to work out a business plan, as you will want to safeguard your own money. The plan may be used to:

- Show to prospective backers to help raise finance.
- Show to landlords to establish your credibility.
- Give business advisers a framework to work on.
- Give you confidence in your ability to succeed.
- Demonstrate that there is a market for your product.

Presenting the plan

Most importantly, the document should be presented in a professional manner. Access to computers and instant print shops means that it is easy and relatively cheap to produce professional-looking documents. You must make every effort to see that your business plan reflects the professional image of the business. By all means use your creative skill to design an interesting cover but let the facts and figures speak for themselves.

Finally, remember that a business plan is not fixed in stone. You may need to make detours if your road ahead is blocked or if another road offers better opportunities. Use it as a working tool, review it constantly and it will prove to be your route to success.

Example of a business plan

Sally Smith Ceramics

Summary

I have completed a BA in Visual Arts, specialising in Ceramics. During my final year, I started to sell my work through a local gallery and believe there is a market for my hand created work. I have therefore decided to set up as a ceramicist and am taking studio space in the local craft centre where I can make and retail my work. I have a small amount of capital and have managed to negotiate a loan. I also intend to apply for Prince's Trust funding. The ceramics that I will produce are individual, one-off pieces with a sculptural quality. My potential market includes collectors, interior designers and consumers with high levels of disposable income.

The Business

I will make and produce individual ceramic pieces for sale through galleries and direct from my workshop. I intend initially sharing a studio in the local craft centre to help keep costs reasonable in the early stages of the business.

I have a degree in Visual Arts and I specialised in ceramics. I intend to use the skills I have developed to produce unusual and innovative sculptural ceramics.

Eventually I would like to have a large studio where I can make and sell my work. I intend at some time in the future to employ people to help me in the business.

I want to have my work on sale in all the major galleries throughout the UK.

The Product

I work in clay using a variety of techniques to create pieces of work. The processes include using slabs of clay to produce tiles which are then wired together. I can also produce more traditional work if required. Many of my pieces are based on Middle Eastern architecture and are often purchased by people because they remind them of their travels.

I believe that my Unique Selling Proposition is that every piece is individual and could not be mass-produced. There is a strong element of innovation in my work and I am constantly experimenting to produce new textures and effects.

Marketing

I have visited many retail outlets to obtain a context and pricing strategy for my work. I have also identified the customer group at which I am aiming. I have talked to established craft workers and designers working in my field, gathering valuable information and advice on starting and running a business. Because every piece I make is different, pricing is difficult but I have identified price points at which I shall aim to produce work. I have also developed a method of calculating the prices of my work.

I intend to hold a launch at the craft centre and to advertise my presence in the local paper. My aunt is the local MP and I am going to ask her to open the studio. I shall send out a press release to promote this event and to mail to existing customers (people who have seen my work at the degree show and other contacts).

I intend to apply to advertise in the *Design Gap* catalogue and set up my own website.

My target markets include:

1. Private and public galleries.
2. Individual consumers who appreciate unusual ceramics and have high levels of disposable income.
3. The corporate market.
4. Interior designers.

I plan to use exhibitions both as a form of initial income and as exposure for my work. Once established at the craft centre, I intend to produce a promotional pack for distribution to galleries, retail outlets and interior designers. I will also submit my work for inclusion on the slide index at the Design Initiative and the Crafts Council slide libraries.

Operational Details

Sharing a studio will inevitably limit production space but will initially cut costs. I have some storage space at home, which I will use to build up stock for exhibitions and Christmas. I will need to purchase a kiln, but shelving and so on is already in place.

The location of the craft centre is in a secondary trading area, but as it has been there for many years it has built up a reputation and many people visit regularly.

I have sourced suppliers for the clay and glazes. I have also received several quotations from carriers for transporting my work.

Finance

I have £1000 in capital and have negotiated loans from my family and the bank to purchase the kiln and provide working capital. A cash flow forecast is attached.

Management

I am confident that I have the skills required to make and sell my work. However, I recognise that I need to improve my business skills and have enrolled on a Business Enterprise course.

The Future

Eventually I should like to have my own studio, preferably in a rural location. I want to establish my reputation as an innovative designer of ceramics and will apply for a stand at the Chelsea Craft Fair and enter other exhibitions and competitions to promote my reputation, both here and abroad.

When funds allow, I will employ someone to help me make my work and employ a part-time bookkeeper.

Reasons given for not writing a business plan

1. BUSINESS PLANS ARE ONLY FOR BIG BUSINESSES

Wrong. Every business, however small, can benefit from having a business plan. The actual process of thinking through every aspect of the business is good discipline for the craftworker. You will be surprised how other ideas will develop and your goals will alter when you consider all the factors involved.

2. I'M TOO BUSY TO WRITE A BUSINESS PLAN
It will save time in the long run. Starting a business is very time-consuming: life becomes hectic and there doesn't seem to be time to do everything. Without a proper plan this state of affairs will continue *ad infinitum*. Writing a plan will help you to identify problems, correct errors, establish priorities and plan the best use of your time.

3. I MIGHT WANT TO CHANGE DIRECTION AT SOME POINT
No problem. A business plan is not unchangeable; it is a tool to work with. By putting down your thoughts on paper you will have something to focus on when new opportunities do arise and the creative abilities flow. You won't be able to take advantage of *all* the opportunities that arise, but working out which ones will fit in with your business plan will help you to remain focused.

4. I DON'T KNOW HOW TO WRITE A BUSINESS PLAN
It's easy. There is no right and wrong way to write a plan. The main person who needs to understand it is YOU. If you are writing a plan for the bank, or to obtain finance, ask if they want it in a special format. Your local Business Link or Enterprise agency will probably be able to help, as will your accountant.

Don't attempt to produce the *perfect* plan, allow yourself a certain amount of time, and work on it in sections. When you have written it, use it, refer to it regularly and keep updating it.

Cash flow

A cash flow is simply a projection of all the money movements involved in the business, i.e. the income and the expenditure. It is a record of when the money is due to come in and go out of your business. Preparing and keeping a cash flow up-to-date allows you to budget properly. You can see at a glance when the bills need paying, if you will need to borrow money and when you can order materials. Producing a cash flow when you first start in business can be quite difficult, but after a year it becomes easier as all you need to do is update the figures.

If you intend to borrow from a bank or seek a loan from the Prince's Trust then one of the first things that they will ask for is a cash flow forecast.

Figures are usually carried out on a monthly basis. At the end of each month the actual figures should replace the projections to update the cash flow. This constant updating means that keeping the cash flow on a computer spreadsheet is a good idea as it allows you to change figures easily. Try and plan your cash flow twelve months in advance. At the end of each month fill in the actual figures.

To compile a cash flow, follow the example on page 34.

Receipts

Work out how much income you expect from sales, and when you expect it to arrive, and enter under Receipts. Also included here should be money received from invoices, fees from other work, VAT collected and capital injected, for example in the form of a loan.

Payments

Calculate the expenses, including your salary, and enter them in on the sheet under Payments. List all the expenses you expect to have to pay each month. This should include all your outgoings. You may have different headings from those on the example, as everyone's business is different.

Learning the skills needed

Acquiring the skills needed to run your own business may seem boring but it is essential to your success. The first step is recognising that you need to increase your skills in a certain area and being prepared to learn how to operate a business. There is plenty of help available, if you know where to look and who to ask.

If you are setting up a studio you may need to borrow money in which case you will need to produce a business plan for the bank. If you don't want to do this yourself, you may need professional help with it. Alternatively, you may just need advice on marketing, how to promote your exhibition or how to keep the books in order. Whatever type of assistance you need, it should be available in your area and some of it will be available free.

Do-It-Yourself

If you prefer to learn things from books and videos, studying at your own pace, there are numerous ones on the market which will help you. Most high street banks offer information packs to their customers starting a business. They are usually also available on CD and can be a good starting point – especially as they are FREE!

The Artist's Newsletter produces a number of handbooks and you may find your local Arts Board also produces information.

Business training courses

If you lack basic business skills then it might be a good idea to attend a business enterprise course. These are known by different names and delivered by a number of organisations. They should provide training in marketing, bookkeeping, dealing with suppliers, and generally give you an insight into running a business. To find the courses available in your area contact your local Enterprise Agency, which should be listed in the telephone directory.

Local help

In recent years there has been a growth in the cultural industries sector, resulting in better advice provision for artists by local authorities. However, this is patchy and is generally more available in areas undergoing regeneration. Schemes such as Loca in Batley, West Yorkshire provide studio space for arts and business seminars to help them sell their work. Some of these organisations are associated with Business Links and Enterprise Agencies and others are connected to the Arts and Museums sector of the local authority, so you may have to do some research to find the appropriate body in your area. If you are struggling, try your local library or your local councillor. If your council does not provide any sort of provision perhaps you should ask 'why not?'

Example cash flow

Month	Start	1	2	3	4	5	6	7	8	9	10	11	12	Total
Income														
Sales		750	800	800	1100	1800	2000	2400	1200	600	900	1500	1300	15150
Own Capital	1750													
Loan	4000													
Total	**5750**	**750**	**800**	**800**	**1100**	**1800**	**2000**	**2400**	**1200**	**600**	**900**	**1500**	**1300**	**20900**
Outgoings														
Purchases	450	70	80	80	100	100	150	150	60	60	70	80	90	1540
Drawings		700	700	700	700	700	700	700	700	700	700	700	700	8400
Wages							400	400						800
Rent and rates		95	95	95	95	95	95	95	95	95	95	95	95	1140
Light, heat and power		25	25	25	25	25	25	35	35	35	35	35	35	360
Telephone		15	15	15	15	15	15	15	15	15	15	15	15	180
Stationery	1100							130						1230
Insurance	150													150
Advertising	1883	35	35	35	35		25	25	25			50	8	2156
Repairs and renewals									125					125
Motor and travel		45	45	45	45	45	45	55	55	55	55	55	55	600
Accounts/solicitors													150	150
Loan repayments								95	95	95	95	95	95	570
Bank charges								5	5	5	5	5	5	30
Purchase of kiln		350				350				350				1050
Capital items	400													400
Total	**3983**	**1335**	**995**	**995**	**1015**	**1330**	**1455**	**1705**	**1210**	**1410**	**1070**	**1130**	**1248**	**18881**
Surplus/Deficit	1767	-585	-195	-195	85	470	545	695	-10	-810	-170	370	52	**2019**
Balance @ Start	0	1767	1182	987	792	877	1347	1892	2587	2577	1767	1597	1967	
Balance @ End	1767	1182	987	792	877	1347	1892	2587	2577	1767	1597	1967	2019	

Chapter 3:

Money Matters

How much finance will you need?

Once you have drawn up a business plan you should be able to work out how much capital you will need to start the business and how much additional funding you will need to finance the cash flow. Raising money needs careful planning, so before you go rushing off to see your bank manager for a loan, check and recheck your figures to make sure that you know *exactly* how much money you need and when you will need it.

Your cash requirements will probably be greater at some times of the year than others and you need to plan for times of greatest need, i.e. when you are carrying the greatest amount of stock or waiting for bills to be paid. Try and steer a middle course: being over-cautious can be as bad as being over-optimistic. Basically, you need money for two purposes:

1. Start-up capital

This is the amount of money that you will need to commence in business. It will include the cost of equipment, vehicles, initial rent of premises, rates, heating bills expected and so on.

2. Working capital

This is the money that will allow you to trade until you are earning sufficient income. This should include an amount to finance the delay between purchasing the materials and selling the product, i.e. to finance your stock during all stages of its progress through the business.

Even if finance is not your strong point you really need to know how it all works if you are to succeed. Control of the finances is the key factor to the success or failure of any business and, if you really don't understand what is going on, either go into business with someone who does or go on a training course!

The amount of working capital that you can raise by borrowing will be limited. If you cannot raise sufficient funds to carry out your plans then they may have to be modified. You could start on a smaller scale, or work from home instead of renting premises, until your business becomes viable. You may need to allow for taking very little salary to begin with.

Investors

You

The main investor in your business will be you; you cannot expect anyone else to lend you money if you are not prepared to invest in it yourself. This can cause problems if, for instance, you have just left college and are short of funds. In this case, you may have to obtain alternative work until you can raise some capital. If you are expecting anyone else to put up some money, the most you can expect is two or three times the size of your own investment. Examine your own financial position carefully: you may have spare cash in the building society or have possessions you can sell - perhaps you could trade down your car? Starting a business demands sacrifices and you cannot expect anyone else to take a risk if you aren't prepared to.

Friends and relatives

The most common way of raising any finance is to borrow from your family. This source of funding is very useful but should be treated with great caution - they may need their money back suddenly and you can then be forced into a difficult situation. You must also prepare for what you will do if the business fails and you need to repay your backers. Would you be able to move house and release some capital?

A loan from friends and relatives could operate in one of the following ways:

1. *Interest-free loan*. Only your nearest and dearest are likely to offer you this. It will probably be short-term i.e. paid back within months rather than years.
2. *Loan with interest*. To avoid disagreement, fix the interest charges when you start. Use an average over the last six months of the bank base rate. This will probably work out cheaper than a loan from the bank or building society.

'Sleeping' partners

Partners will need to be more aware of the activities of the business, and they should also be aware of their liability for any debts. Although they are unlikely to be concerned with the day-to-day running of the business, they will certainly want to keep in touch with the way it is run. They will not draw a wage but will be entitled to a percentage of the profits proportional to their investment.

Other sources of funding

Grants

You may be able to obtain grants, allowances, cheap loans or awards from a variety of sources. Contact your local Arts Board to find out whether there are any schemes set up in your area. Your other first point of contact should be the local Business Link. They operate a variety of schemes. If you are prepared to relocate, then look at what is available in other areas. For instance, Birmingham has an excellent record for encouraging and supporting small businesses. If you are between the ages of 18 and 30, the Prince's Trust offers grants if you cannot raise the finance from other sources and the Shell Livewire competition offers similar help.

Bank loans

Borrowing money from the bank is expensive, so be careful to work out your best option. Consider the financial markets when negotiating a loan. A fixed interest rate loan is good when interest rates are low but can be a millstone when rates are high and then fall. Make sure you fully recognise those circumstances when the bank could pull the (financial) rug from under you. Never sign any undertaking of which you do not understand the possible consequences.

START-UP LOANS

Businesses that have been trading for less than twelve months are often eligible for start-up loans. These can be very flexible and allow you to control when you pay them back. The availability of these and the rates on offer change all the time, so check with the bank for any special deals or schemes.

BUSINESS DEVELOPMENT LOANS

This is the type of loan you will need if you are a growing business or going to purchase a major piece of equipment. These have fixed interest rates and fixed monthly repayments. Once again, shop around, as different banks will offer different deals. This is often a cheaper way of buying a vehicle than a deal from a car showroom.

BUSINESS OVERDRAFT

If the need for money is likely to be fairly short term, an overdraft is likely to be your best option. Overdrafts are relatively cheap to arrange and flexible, but they will only cover part of your financial requirements. The bank may require some type of security, usually in the form of a personal guarantee. Most businesses operate with some type of overdraft facility but make sure that you agree a limit with the bank and stick to it, as unauthorised overdrafts are generally very expensive. The main advantage of an overdraft is that you do not pay interest when you do not use it. The disadvantages are that the interest rate is variable and that the bank can demand repayment instantly.

Small Firms Loan Guarantee scheme

This is a loan scheme guaranteed by the Government for businesses without security or a track record. You can pay this loan back over two to ten years and choose between a fixed or variable interest rate. You also pay a premium to the Government. Details of how to apply may be obtained from banks or the DTI.

Small Firms Training loan

This is a loan for businesses to help pay for training costs. You can borrow between £500 and £125,000 and pay the loan back over one to seven years. Interest payments will be paid by the Government for the first 26, 39 or 52 weeks, depending on the amount borrowed. Again, contact your bank or the DTI for further deatils.

Choosing a bank

There is a lot of help available for businesses from financial institutions and business advisers, all of whom are competing for your custom. Most banks offer some incentive to win your custom. Free banking for a year is a common one, but make sure that the bank is one you will want to be with long term as changing banks can involve a lot of paperwork.

Increasingly, financial assistance from the banks is being tied to training. For instance, at least one high street bank offers free banking for eighteen months if you have been on a business training course run by a recognised training agency. This can save you a lot of money, as bank charges are generally very high, so it's worth investigating.

Types of account

Most businesses operate with two types of account:

1. *Business account.* These generally offer a full range of banking services, including cheque books, paying-in books, monthly statements, standing orders, direct debits and various types of service card. It is always advisable, and sometimes necessary, to set up a business account as it is more professional to keep your personal and business finances separate. When you are starting up you should be able to find free banking of some sort.
2. *Reserve account.* This is an instant access account to which you can transfer your spare (!) cash to accumulate interest. The interest rate paid is usually fairly minimal so, if you do have large amounts of cash spare, it will probably be better off in a building society account. Reserve accounts can, however, be a good way of saving for the rent or the telephone bill, or anything else that is paid quarterly.

Tax and self-assessment

Everyone has to pay tax on their earnings, whether they are employed or self-employed. Companies must produce accounts for the Inland Revenue to agree and charge tax correctly when appropriate. Since you need an accountant to look over your record books and prepare these, I will not go into more detail here. For people who are self-employed, the system is known as self-assessment. This system makes you responsible for keeping such records as are needed to allow you to make a complete and correct tax return.

The system in the UK is that when you first become self-employed you should inform the Inland Revenue. They will send you a notification form to register as a self-employed person. They will then send you a tax return to fill in. This consists of a 'core' return, plus additional pages for other sources of income, such as employment income, partnership income and so on. There is a booklet which comes with the tax return giving advice on how to complete it. Do read this carefully.

When you fill in your tax return you can decide whether you want to calculate the tax yourself or ask the Inland Revenue to do it. If you want the Inland Revenue to calculate it you must return your form by the 30th September. Either way – just as with a company – professional advice may be necessary.

Paying tax

The Inland Revenue will send you a statement of account shortly before payments are due. Payments are made in three stages:

1. The balance of tax for the previous year is payable by the 31st January following the end of the tax year.
2. The first instalment of tax on account for the next year is also payable on 31st January.
3. The second instalment of tax on account for the next year is payable the following 31st July.

It is really important that your forms and payments arrive on time as the Inland Revenue has the power to impose penalties and interest charges on late payment. If you discover that you have made an error in your tax return you can amend this by writing to the Inspector of Taxes any time up to a year after the filing date.

If you are worried about anything then ring the Inland Revenue help desk and ask. If you are really worried about handling this yourself then go to an accountant. As long as your books are in order, it won't take him a long time to fill in the form and may save you money in the long run.

National Insurance

You will also need to notify the National Insurance office that you are now self-employed and contract to pay the right contributions. It is important to do this as it can affect your pension rights. If you have a very low income you can decide to opt out, but it may not be in your best interests.

Pensions

The stakeholder pension is designed for those on low incomes. If you do not have any pension provision it is worth considering. Depending on your age, ISAs and other saving schemes may prove a more flexible alternative. It is a good idea to discuss this with your accountant or an Independent Financial Adviser.

Mortgages

It is a myth that you can't get a 'normal' mortgage if you're self-employed; however, it is more difficult. Lenders are becoming increasingly aware of different working patterns. While most maintain that they do not treat the self-employed any differently, you are likely to find that they do require two years' certified accounts to show that you can afford the mortgage. However, some will lend on 'self-certification', i.e. you give income figures without having to prove them. To take this route, you will need a substantial deposit and will probably have to pay a higher rate of interest. Another alternative is to find someone willing to guarantee your mortgage, such as a parent.

If you are buying commercial premises then you will need a commercial mortgage and different conditions will apply. The best advice is to shop around, contact various lenders and ask them for their opinions. Search for money advice on one of the money websites on the Internet, or contact one of the organisations for the self-employed and ask for their advice.

Top tip

Before you become self-employed, try to save enough money to keep you going for three months in case of emergency. Put it in a separate bank account and don't touch it: it's amazing what a feeling of security it gives you.

Chapter 4:

The Product

The most exciting part of running a craft business is making something that satisfies your creativity and then finding someone who likes it so much that they want to buy it. This is guaranteed to give you a real buzz! If you are already working in your craft and are competent enough to produce saleable goods then you have to find out what will sell in the marketplace to earn a living.

Crafts

In a craft business, product design is something that is constantly evolving. Almost every day new ideas will occur and you will always be testing out the possibilities of changing designs and improving your work.

In order to compete with mass-produced goods your product needs to be 'different'. It needs to find a 'niche' to succeed.

'Bread and butter' line

Most craftworkers find that they need a bread and butter line to survive. These are lines that are easy to produce and sell well. For example, a leather worker who makes briefcases may also make belts as a bread and butter line.

A silkscreen artist may have his designs made up as cards.

Checklist of marketing potential for craftwork

1. Does it appeal to a small but accessible group of people?
2. Does part of the process involve handcrafting, something that needs your exclusive talent?
3. Will the skill, time and effort that go into its production be reflected in the price?
4. Do you use materials that are difficult for large manufacturers to use? (Many craftworkers have succeeded by using recycled materials as part of their products.)
5. Is there a niche market for your product?

If you can answer yes to the above, then you should have a good chance of success. Remember: the work of individual craftworkers should be instantly recognisable – you need to develop a very distinctive style which collectors recognise.

Developing a product range

Producing a range of products which relate to each other can increase sales by inspiring people to collect. Start by examining and considering the designs that you are currently making. Try and assess if any modifications need to be made to make them saleable, and what new products could be designed to fit into a range.

As a craftworker, product design will be a part of your work but you should try and build some time into your working week when you can experiment. Carry a notebook with you everywhere and try out new ideas on friends, buyers and fellow craftworkers.

To be successful you need to be constantly improving and innovating. When designing a product you need to consider exactly what it is that makes customers buy the product. Do they *need* a jug or a gift, or are they collecting craftwork and enjoy the image of having craft items around the house? By working out why your customers buy your products you should be able to increase sales.

Unique Selling Proposition

The Unique Selling Proposition is what makes your product different from anyone else's, and it also adds value to your product. Adding value to a product is the way of making sure that it is your product rather than your competitor's that succeeds. Because of the nature of craftwork, most craft businesses already have a Unique Selling Proposition, but if you think that yours could be improved then try one of the ideas below.

- Produce a limited edition and give every piece a certificate.
- Add extra features.
- If you're the first to produce something, tell everyone.
- Sign your pieces.
- Improve your point of sale material. Give written details of the product, its history, materials used, etc.
- Be the best.
- Find a historical link.
- Find a celebrity link.
- Promote regional significance.
- Give guarantees and warranties.

Evaluating a new product

To find out if a product is right for the marketplace, carry out some simple market research. When you design a new product, evaluate it yourself. Asking other people to give it a score out of five on each of the following aspects will help you to compare it with existing products:

- Appeal.
- Appearance.
- Cost.
- Design.
- Technique.
- Uniqueness.
- Usefulness.

You should also evaluate it on the following grounds:

- Availability of materials.
- Hours of labour.
- Profitability.

The lifecycle of a product

Few products go on selling forever without any updating or modifications. Sales will generally peak and then start to decline. The way to monitor this properly is to keep records so that, when a product declines, you can cut back on production or re-evaluate the product, rather than keep stockpiling something which is not selling. You will often hear a puzzled craftworker saying, 'But I've been selling it for years,' when sales start to drop off. Remember that tastes and fashion change and this is true in crafts as well as other businesses.

Health and Safety

Whatever type of product you make, always ensure that it conforms to Health and Safety regulations. If you are in any doubt then check with your local Trading Standards Officer (the address will be in your local telephone book).

Artwork

Trying to earn a living with original artwork is very difficult. Even artists who earn thousands of pounds for each painting can struggle. There is a limited market for original works of art and if you wish to develop a reputation and earn an income you may need to look for other methods of promoting your work.

Prints, postcards and greetings cards

One way of earning money and increasing your profile is by selling your designs as prints, cards and postcards. This is becoming increasingly popular as improved methods of printing are bringing the cost down and making it affordable.

Obviously, reproducing paintings in this way suits some type of work more than others, but it is possible to sell abstract work, for example, as postcards, as well as local landscapes, provided you go for the right market.

If you exhibit regularly at art fairs and markets you may find it useful to have a range of these printed products. Many people who admire your work may not be able to afford an original but by buying a card may well remember you in the future and this can lead to commissions – provided, of course, that you remember to print a contact number on the back!

PRINTS

Prints are reproductions of your work. They can be sold unmounted, mounted or framed. They can be sold through galleries and art shops. A number of artists are also reporting growing success by selling over the Internet, where customers seem prepared to risk spending £50 on a print where they wouldn't spend £500 on an unseen original. To see what is available and the sort of prices they charge, scroll through the websites of the galleries advertised in the back of art magazines.

LIMITED EDITION PRINTS

Limited edition prints are those where the artist guarantees that only a certain number will be produced. These can be as few as five for an etching or up to 500 for a print of a watercolour. Although the prints need not all be produced at once in order to save money, the artist must make sure that only the correct number is produced. Each print has to be signed and numbered, being the artist's guarantee of authenticity. Some artists underestimate the interest that there will be in their print and produce a limited edition of 50 only to find that they could have sold more, which is very frustrating. Prints often keep selling for a number of years, so take this into account when calculating how many to produce. If you are selling at a fair it is a good idea to take a framed print for display and then to sell the others packaged either flat or in a cardboard tube. Sometimes people charge more money for the first print, as it is considered special. At one time, a print run was very expensive but, with modern paper and printing equipment, it is possible to produce your own. Alternatively, contact the printers advertised in art magazines.

Postcards

Postcards are popular and easy to sell but do not usually generate a lot of income because of their low selling price. They are, however, really useful for developing a reputation and thereby bringing in commissions. They can also be framed to make small pictures. There are huge differences in cost on postcards, depending on quality and quantity. In tourist areas, quality postcards generally find a good market for people who want something different in the way of local scenes. In university towns there is usually a good market for postcards of any subject amongst the student population.

Greetings cards

If you are planning to sell greetings cards into a shop then you will need a good range. Few shops want to be bothered with half a dozen cards - they need enough to make a display so you may have to make a considerable investment. If you are able to sell them yourself alongside your work at shows and markets, then you will probably find that they are a good source of income. It is possible to produce short print runs using a home computer or a local print shop.

Original cards are very popular and can be very profitable. As with everything else, presentation is important. Greetings cards need to be cellophane-wrapped with an envelope and labelled professionally.

Display

If you are selling your work through shops or galleries then produce a small display card advertising the work.

Draw attention to the fact that it was created by an artist and not mass-produced. Shops always welcome point of sale material, provided it is professionally produced, but do leave a space for the shop to put their own prices. A proper display stand should also increase your sales. These can be purchased from shop fitters listed in Yellow Pages.

Chapter 5:

Finding the Space

Working from home

Most craftworkers start off working from home. The fact that there is no rent to pay and that they can work at odd hours makes it very convenient. Unfortunately, not everyone has the space to do this. Some people find it difficult to concentrate on their work in the home environment and for those who work on a large scale or need special equipment it may be essential for them to find a larger space. If you are fortunate enough to have an outbuilding or spare room this could be a viable option for you.

Officially, anyone operating a business from home needs to have planning permission. In reality, if you are operating at a fairly low level of production and not causing a nuisance to your neighbours you will probably be ignored. However, it is always advisable to operate legally. Trading without planning permission could mean that your insurance is invalid, and failure to give information on business stock kept at home may mean that your home contents insurance policy provides insufficient cover. You may also be in breach of your tenancy or mortgage agreement.

To obtain planning permission, contact the planning department of your local council and tell them what you propose. They are generally very helpful, although you are unlikely to obtain retail planning permission for a residential property.

Setting up a studio

If you do decide to look for a studio or workshop then, before you start, you need to decide what it is you require. All sorts of issues will affect the space you rent: size, location, facilities, proximity to customers and, of course, cost.

Some things you might like to consider include:

- Is living accommodation required or workspace alone?
- Are you prepared to share?
- Where do you want to be situated?
- What size space do you need? (Don't forget to allow for growth.)
- Will you require 24 hour access to the space?
- What facilities do you need? (Electricity, gas, water etc.)
- How secure do the premises need to be?
- Do you have any special requirements? (Is your work noisy? Do you need ground floor access?)
- And, most important, what can you afford? Don't forget to allow for any premiums required to buy the lease. You may need a solicitor and there may be work required before you move in. Remember bargains are not always what they seem, unofficial cheap space may seem great but if you have to move every six months it may prove expensive in the long run.

Finding a studio

Finding a studio is not always an easy thing to do. In inner cities, where workspace used to be cheap and easily available, artists are being moved out of their studios to make way for loft apartments. Your first port of call should be your local estate agent. One that handles commercial properties is the most likely to have suitable premises.

If you are part of the local craft network, you may find that you hear of opportunities before they are advertised. Sometimes you can share a studio, and some landlords have several properties that they rent out. Your local Arts Board will have a list of group studios in the area and many councils have a Cultural Development Officer who may be able to help. If you are going to share, remember that fine artists and craftworkers do not always make easy bedfellows. If you produce textiles or fine art then you will not want to be in a studio with dusty potters!

You can also advertise on notice boards, particularly at the local art school or in art shops and in magazines such as *The Craftsman* or *The Artist's Newsletter*. If all this fails, then walk round potential areas looking for boards and empty property. Your local council should know who owns a property, if the neighbours don't. Obvious possibilities are space above shops, or places that people don't want to live in, like top floors of warehouses, disused buildings such as churches, schools, factories and so on. Don't consider squatting – it's no way to run a business.

How much can I afford?

When working out what you can afford don't forget that there are both running costs and capital costs. Capital costs are one-off expenses, such as alterations to the roof, floor and walls, installation of fireproofing or fire doors, re-wiring, plumbing, and purchasing fixtures from the landlord or existing tenant, e.g. a kiln.

Running costs include the rent, general rates, water rates, insurance, any service charge such as caretaking or group advertising, minor repairs, gas and electricity, telephone and the cost of transport from home to studio.

Negotiating with a landlord

Having found your premises, the next step is to negotiate with the landlord. In areas where space is at a premium, there will probably be little room for manoeuvre but if you are renting a difficult-to-let property then you may be able to negotiate. It's always worth making an offer, particularly if you are being asked an unusually high amount. Rents are usually quoted in square metres or feet per year, for example 20m × 15m at £4 per square metre. Before making an agreement with a landlord, check that he will allow you to make any structural changes to the property that you may require.

Contracts

For most premises you will have to sign some sort of lease. All written or verbal negotiations should be conducted on a 'subject to contract' basis. These words will appear at the top of all letters and correspondence. If you are handling the negotiations yourself then you should include them. This means that you can withdraw at any time until the final contract is exchanged.

Do make sure that the property is suitable for the use

that you want; if the premises are designated for storage only then you would be working illegally and, although change of use can be applied for through the local planning office, it is not always granted.

Licence

Occasionally you may be offered space on 'licence'. This usually means sharing the space. Your rights are limited and you are usually on a flexible contract with a termination period of one month if paying monthly.

It is always advisable to seek legal advice before signing any sort of lease.

Group workshops and craft centres

In the last few years there has been a substantial growth in studio provision at craft centres. The visual arts officer at the local Arts Board should have a list of premises in your area currently available. Some of these are open to the public all the time - others only open for exhibitions. If they are open all the time, make sure you will have sufficient time to produce the goods as well as serving the public. There should always be one day when you are not expected to open. Some have joint display space staffed by someone else, which can be a useful way of allowing you to get on with your work.

When looking for a craft centre check the following:

- What are the opening times?
- Are there opportunities for joint publicity?
- Who runs it? (Paid staff or a committee of craftworkers?)

- Will you be expected to take on a share in the running?
- Will there be exhibitions?
- Will you have access to other facilities, like a photocopier or computers?
- Is the location favourable?
- What is the length of the tenancy? (Can you exit quickly?)
- Who are the other tenants? (Is there a mix or is it biased towards one craft?)

Finding a suitable location

Have you ever wondered why a business succeeds in one area yet fails in another? Why do craftworkers thrive in some parts of the country and not in others? In some businesses, such as retailing, it is obvious that you need to be situated in a popular shopping area with plenty of passing trade. With other businesses the importance of location is not always apparent yet being in the right place can be crucial to the success of your business. The problem of where to locate your business is just as important to small businesses as it is to large organisations. The area must have the right type of customer. It is no use setting up a high-class gallery in an area of high unemployment.

A complete change?

People who want a complete change of lifestyle often decide to relocate in order to start a business. Many people dream of living and working in the country or moving to their favourite holiday town. If you are planning to move and start a business investigate the area carefully. A town which is busy in summer may be dead for six months of the year.

Many craftworkers and artists have moved to parts of the country where housing is cheap without considering why it is cheap. The usual reason is that people living in that particular area do not have much disposable income compared with other parts of the country. This often means that there are no customers locally and you may have to travel long distances to find craft fairs and galleries from which to sell your goods. The cost of doing this may well outweigh the cheaper living costs.

Making the decision

If you are already running a business, moving premises may be the first big step you take. It is easy to fall into the trap of many small business owners by considering the size, type, suitability and running cost of the premises before their location. The right way is to look at the location first and then to consider the property available.

So how do you find the right location? Firstly, by deciding what is important to your business. Consider the following factors:

- *Access to markets.* How close do you need to be to your customers? Are the right types of people living in the area?
- *Availability of grants and subsidies.* Some areas can award a wide range of grants and subsidies to businesses moving into the area. If this could affect you, check with your local Business Link or Enterprise Agency.
- *Proximity to suppliers.* If you rely on frequent deliveries from a supplier, would it make sense to locate close to them?

- *Cost.* Rent and rates may vary considerably.
- *Communications and roads.* Do you need to be close to the motorway network or adjacent to a railway station?
- *Environment.* Do you want to live and work in the country or is a town centre more appropriate for your business?

When you find a location use the following checklist to compare locations.

- Proximity to customers.
- Number of competitors in the area.
- Rent and rates.
- Convenience for transport.
- Ease of access.
- Attractiveness of area.
- Availability of parking.
- Cost and availability of insurance.
- Availability of staff.
- Security.

The 'feel right' factor

As any business owner will tell you, it is also important to consider the 'feel right' factor. Many successful businesses have been started in unlikely places because it 'felt right'. This doesn't mean that you must ignore everything else. Carrying out an investigation as listed above will give you the knowledge necessary to make an informed decision and hopefully it will also 'feel right'!

Let people know where you are!

If selling from your studio you need to ensure that people can find their way to the business. Always provide a good location map preceding a customer visit. Ensure that the studio is well signposted and that details of car parking are provided. Planning authorities should be consulted before erecting signs on the public highway or in conservation areas. Other regulations concerning illuminated signs and so on vary from area to area.

Chapter 6:

Keeping Control

Basic administration

Every business requires some basic 'paperwork'. Your accounts need to be up-to-date, your cash flow calculated and details of your customers, orders and so on readily available. It may seem a waste of time when you are starting a business and trying to do twenty things at once, but keeping everything in order and easily accessible will actually save you time. Put your systems in place before you start your business, and set aside a regular time each week to bring everything up-to-date, and you will make life easier for yourself and run your business more efficiently.

Office equipment

You do not need a special room in which to do your paperwork but you need some space in your studio or home where you can keep everything together. Second-hand office suppliers sell things like filing cabinets, usually at a reasonable cost. Access to a computer is virtually essential in order to provide a professional image for invoices, letters and for access to the Internet. A computer with a design package can save you money as you can print your own leaflets. There are various deals available on refurbished computers so think about what you really need and then try and find the cheapest way of obtaining the equipment.

Checklist for basic office equipment:

- Desk or table.
- Chair.
- Filing cabinet (this really will make life so much easier so find a second-hand one if you can't buy new).
- Telephone with an answering machine (so you don't miss orders).
- Fax machine (once thought of as a luxury but rapidly becoming a necessity).
- Access to a word processor or computer.
- Lever arch files.
- Files and boxes.
- Invoice/order books.
- Paper.
- Stapler, paper clips, hole punch, pens etc.
- IN and OUT tray.

When you purchase these don't worry about image at this stage. Go for value - no-one will see them and they don't make you any money!

Stationery

You will need:

- Letterheaded paper. This can be used for invoices, statements and letters. If you are going to use a lot then you can have it printed separately, or you can design something on your computer.

- Business cards. These are essential. You can make your own, so don't buy expensive ones – the more you give out the better.
- Compliments slips. Surprisingly useful and they save letterheads.

Many printers offer an inclusive deal to new businesses so shop around.

- Envelopes. Buy the cheapest available in a variety of sizes.

Controlling the cash

Many people create difficulties for themselves by mixing business money with their personal cash. If you don't keep proper records, you will run into trouble when you have to produce annual accounts or fill in self-assessment forms. This can end up costing a lot of money.

Cash boxes

Keep a cash box for business money. If you don't need a till, jot down every time you take money out or put it in. Keep every single receipt filed away carefully, as they can be claimed against tax. The simplest system consists of an account book, like a Simplex D, Everite or something similar, available from any good stationer's.

Files

File bills away as they come in using dividers to keep everything in month order so it's easy to see what you owe and what is owed to you. Use the four file system for ease. This consists of four lever arch files:

1. Purchase invoices you receive for goods you purchase. Transfer when paid to . . .
2. Purchase invoices paid.
3. Sales invoices you send out to your customers. Transfer when paid to . . .
4. Sales invoices paid.

You will also need a separate file for bank statements. Keep a file for orders, either filed monthly or under each customer. Transfer to another file when completed. Don't throw them away as the customer might want to repeat the order. *Every year, start new files.*

Chapter 7:

The Customer

Who are your customers?

This may seem like a simple question but it is in fact the crux of your business. The customer is the person who makes the business: try staying in business without anyone buying your products and you won't last very long! Since the customer is so important, it is in your interests to find out as much about him as possible.

If you have not yet started trading, you may have to try and visualise your customer. You can do this by:

- *Creating a visual picture.* Buy a magazine of the type you think your customer will purchase, and cut out images which you feel reflect your customer. Create a collage and put this in a prominent place so that you will remember for whom you are making you product.
- *Creating a word association.* Try describing your customer in words. The following descriptions could be applied to different types of customers who would buy different products: rich and rustic; budget conscious with ethnic taste; modern and mobile.

When you know who your customers are then your business becomes more effective. You can target your advertising better and go to fairs where they are likely to visit. Your craftwork can also grow with your customers. If, for example, you are targeting the student market, you can decide to stay with that or you can decide to change your style to suit them when they start to settle down and their tastes and needs alter.

You may attract different customers if you produce a number of ranges but beware of trying to appeal to all tastes. Don't expect all your customers to fit your profile: there will always be the exception but, to be a success, you need to produce for the majority, not the exception.

Once you have a clear idea of your customer then you can consider the limitations of your market. If you are designing lampshades suitable for an interior designer to use in wine bars you will clearly have a limited market; if you can also design a range suitable for selling to individuals then you will target a different market and increase your chances of success.

Customer care

Many artists and craftworkers worry that they are not very good at selling. Arts and crafts are not like double-glazing: the hard sell is unlikely to be necessary and, in fact, can be counter-productive. Treat your customers with due respect and, if you are making the right product at the right price, they will buy. Customers need to feel valued. They need to feel that you will notice if they stop buying from you, so be friendly, show them appreciation and they will return.

The ten golden rules for customer care are:

1. Smile every time you greet a customer.

2. Never ignore customers; speak to them as soon as possible, even if it is to ask them to wait.
3. Always apologise for any delay.
4. Never talk to a friend rather than a customer.
5. If you cannot help, suggest someone who can.
6. Install an answering machine if you are retailing so that you don't have to leave a customer or ever miss a sale.
7. Never criticise one customer to another.
8. Don't react if the customer is less than complimentary; he might just be having a bad day.
9. Don't let it show if you don't like a customer. Many artists are very proprietary about their work and only like it to go to good homes – this is not good business.
10. If you want information, ask politely. 'Please' and 'thank you', 'hello' and 'goodbye' cost nothing.

Increasing customer loyalty

Everyone likes a gift. A free key-ring from a leatherworker, or even a free pen with your name and number on it will be appreciated and will act as a reminder of your work. A postcard depicting an artist's work will remind a potential buyer of the type of work you produce and your address.

Consumer rights

Contrary to popular opinion, customers do not have an automatic right to a refund. It is obviously a good idea to exchange goods, if possible, as this increases customer satisfaction. However, legally you only have to refund a customer's money if the goods supplied are faulty, not fit for the purpose or not as described.

Creating a customer database

Building and using a customer database is one of the most useful marketing tools for a craftworker. A computer is the ideal storage medium for a database, particularly if it prints labels, but it is possible to keep a database on a card index system.

Start collecting names and addresses as soon as possible. You'll need to ask people's permission, but they are generally happy to let you write to them. The most useful people to have on your list are the people who have bought from you in the past, as well as those who have made enquiries but not yet placed an order. Useful contacts to add to your mailing list include:

- Media contacts.
- Members of arts associations.
- Gallery owners (you can use Yellow Pages, directories or publications from Arts Councils, etc. to find addresses).

You can build up your own mailing list by keeping a list of your own customers and research new ones by using Yellow Pages or Trade Directories. This is the cheapest method but it will take time and may not prove to be cost effective. It is also important to update the list regularly, eliminating 'gone aways' and 'died' from your list. When you make a sale, always ask the customer for his name and address. Occasionally someone might refuse, but it's not very likely. At fairs, have a clipboard on your stall for people to put their names on if they want you to send them details. If you make it clear that you will not pass on their details to anyone else, then people are usually quite happy to add their name. When attending any function or trade fair always ask people for a business card as this will form the basis for your list of contacts. Sometimes artists pool their resources and do a joint mailing and share mailing list contacts.

You can buy a mailing list from a mailing list company, but unfortunately you can only use this once and it is unlikely to be as effective as one you've built yourself. The cost will depend on the quality of the list and how current it is. Prices are normally quoted in terms of £s per hundred names. Renting a list is becoming increasingly common as an independent mailing house carries out the actual mailing using your promotional material, saving you time and, in theory, money.

Mailing lists often suffer from duplicate or obsolete names and addresses, so always buy or rent from a reliable source. To find a mailing list, consult *BRAD Direct Marketing* at your local library. It lists over 4,000 business and consumer mailing lists available for rental. There are also list brokers who can advise on the type of list for your purpose. Locally, you may be able to borrow a list from another business or organise a joint promotion. For instance, a potter may swap lists with a jeweller or wood turner.

If you keep your mailing list on computer then you need to register with the Data Protection Registrar (see the Resource File, page 165).

Using the database

You can use your database to inform your customers about:

- Craft fairs you are attending.
- Forthcoming exhibitions.
- New products.
- Successes and awards.

Newsletters can be a very effective means of promotion, providing a link between craftworker and customer. They can be used to advertise your presence at shows, to launch new products, or to remind customers of your range. Newsletters are relatively inexpensive to produce and can be distributed to those on your mailing list, given to customers at craft fairs and included with orders.

Your customers, whether wholesale or retail, will generally be interested in any developments you make in your product range, and it is often easier for them to assimilate the information through a newsletter rather than a price list.

Include personal information if you enjoy having a social relationship with your customers. Many of them become friends over the years and do like to keep in touch. Some of the best newsletters involve the customers in the business by sharing details that they wouldn't have otherwise known.

Producing a newsletter couldn't be simpler. The advent of personal computers and desktop publishing packages has made it easy for anyone to produce professional looking newsletters at low cost. Photocopying is widely available at very reasonable prices. If possible, use slightly heavier paper quality than is usually available – it does improve the appearance of the newsletter and costs very little extra.

Use illustrations where possible. You could use some of the images available free of copyright on graphics packages, or find someone who can scan in an illustration or, if all else fails, paste the illustration on after you have written the newsletter, before photocopying. Remember, you will need permission before making use of any already published material.

Newsletters are most effective if produced on a regular basis: every three months is a good interval, unless you have something special to announce. You can include special offers, discount vouchers or even carry advertising for fellow craftworkers to help with the cost. Details of interesting commissions, exhibitions, prizes won or the use of new materials are all of interest to your customers. If you find it difficult to think of something to write about, think of the type of questions you are asked at craft fairs - this is the type of information that is most likely to appeal to your readers.

Chapter 8:

Where to Sell Your Work

Reaching your customers

You will probably have to use a variety of methods to reach your customers. You may be able to sell direct from your workshop or studio, your product might be suitable for selling by mail order, or you could market your work over the Internet. Whatever method you use it is always useful to meet customers face to face, either at craft fairs or art markets. The feedback you will get is invaluable.

Craft fairs

One of the main outlets for craftwork is through craft fairs. These vary greatly in their size, quality and ability to draw the customers. The most prestigious event is the annual Chelsea Craft Fair organised by the Crafts Council. It is judged and the standards are very high. It is undoubtedly the fair to which most craftworkers aspire, but it is very difficult to be accepted to show there, particularly for newcomers.

Around the country there is a wide variety of fairs, which vary in quality and size. You need to be very careful when choosing a fair. Sometimes fairs which are billed as craft fairs actually allow people to sell bought-in goods.

This is causing concern generally within the industry and creates problems for the genuine craftworker. The advent of specialist fairs has improved the situation and the market generally.

Beginners often fail to recognise that there are many variations on the craft fair and that they must target their market in exactly the same way as if they were advertising or selling to shops. Visiting as many craft fairs as possible is essential. Talk to the stallholders who are already exhibiting, as they are usually very helpful. Watch what people are buying. Do the customers match your customer profile?

Craft fair organisers

The various events around the country are organised by different organisers; some stage national events and others organise them mainly in their own area. You will probably want to start locally to find your feet. However, do try and avoid the amateur craft fair, as it is unlikely to attract the type of customer you require. Go to a fair organised by one of the recognised organisers listed in the Resource File, page 169. The experience that you will gain at your first fair will be invaluable, even if you do not sell much of your work.

Choosing a fair

There is no foolproof way of choosing a good fair. A fair that is really successful one year may be a disaster the next due to the weather or the fact that a new attraction has been sited in the area. In addition, many small craft fair organisers start up at venues that are too small or so out of the way that they fail to attract sufficient customers.

There is much debate about craft fairs which allow the resale of 'bought-in goods'. Most craft fair organisers will state that they do not allow this type of stall but, if they have last minute cancellations or poor bookings, they are often tempted to allow this type of trader in rather than have an empty space. Organisers maintain that this is preferable to cancelling the show for everyone's sake. It can, however, be very frustrating if you are selling real craftwork to be placed next to someone selling cheap imported goods. There is little you can do about it except to avoid those organisers in the future. You can help the organisers by not cancelling your stall at the last minute because you do not have enough products; this is a frequent complaint of organisers, particularly during the Christmas period.

How to apply for a stand

Many craft shows book up twelve months in advance and it may take you time to get into the show you want. Having decided which shows you want to apply for, write to the organisers and ask for details and a list of venues. Some organisers request a stamped addressed envelope for information and a booking form. A good organiser will always ask to see samples of your work; at the very least they should ask to see photographs, or for details of where you have previously exhibited. Photographs will need to be of good quality.

Professional organisers want to present as good a show as possible and, if they turn you down, try and find out why. They should also try and provide a wide variety of crafts at each show so, if they refuse you at one show, they may well offer you an alternative venue.

When filling in the forms do read the small print where the Terms and Conditions are stated. These should include details of:

- What happens in the event of a show being cancelled.
- What happens if you cancel your stall.
- Fire safety regulations.
- Insurance requirements.
- When you can set up and pack away.
- Any details about demonstrating.

Cost of a stall

Generally, space is booked in units of 6′ × 2′ tables. A basic 6′ table can cost anything from £20 to £100 or more for a day, depending on the venue and the number of customers expected. Obviously, what you receive for £100 will be more than you will get for £20. If you want to exhibit at a top venue with tens of thousands of visitors, then you will need to be prepared to pay for the privilege. Initially, rents might seem high but two days' rent of a craft stall, if it provides all your income, may be equivalent to a week's shop rent and rates. Remember, if the organisers do not charge sufficient rent they will not have the money available to advertise widely and promote the event properly.

What do you get for the money?

The stand fee will include the hire of a table, two chairs and a power supply for lights. Sometimes electricity is charged as an extra so do check; just occasionally it may not even be supplied which could prove disastrous.

If there is the opportunity to advertise in a brochure make sure they have your details and, if they ask for information, make sure that you give it to them in time for publication. Similarly, if you want to demonstrate, make sure that you will be allowed to and that you will have enough room. Some organisers encourage demonstrations and will allow you more space or give you some free publicity.

Before the show

A good organiser will supply you with all the necessary information about setting-up times, opening times for the public, how to reach the venue, unloading and parking arrangements. This is particularly important at city venues. At shows like Chelsea you have very little time to unload and everything is timed with precision. Don't forget to book accommodation in plenty of time. If it's out of term time, student accommodation can be a good option.

The organiser may also send you some publicity material to distribute. Use it! The more visitors that arrive, the greater your chance of success. If you have a list of customers, don't forget to let them know that you will be showing at a certain event.

Insurance

Most event organisers require you to insure for Public Liability claims. Sometimes they will include a form for insurance when you apply for a stand. It is important to be properly insured at events and also to ensure that your goods are insured when being transported, or if stored in your van overnight.

Arriving at the show

There should be a plan displayed giving details of your stand, or there may be someone to greet you or book you in. If you are not sure, then ask. Don't worry about being the newcomer - everyone has to start somewhere and it will often appear chaotic and confusing to the beginner.

Your stand

The standards of display seen at craft fairs are increasingly professional. Basic etiquette demands that your table is covered on three sides and that no packing boxes can be seen. If you want to make an impact you will have to go further than this. See page 110 for advice on display.

Don't block access to your neighbours' stands or try to take over their area - this really will cause problems. All organisers ask that your stand is ready to go, with all boxes cleared from the walkways, well in advance of opening.

It's always a good idea to take someone with you to help with the loading and unloading, and to allow you to have a coffee break. If you must eat on the stand, do it discreetly. The sight of someone munching a sandwich is not the type of professional image you are aiming for.

It is important to create a good impression on your customers. Make sure that everything you sell is labelled and include a price list with all purchases. Occupy your time by doing something related to your work, rather than reading the paper. Always smile and greet potential customers in a friendly manner.

Personal appearance

Although no one expects a craftworker selling at a craft fair to wear a formal suit, it is important to wear the right clothes for the right occasions and your appearance should reflect the quality of your products. Only very successful artists and craftworkers can afford to be eccentric. Be neat and tidy at all times and, if appropriate, wear your own goods.

Art fairs and markets

Over the past few years there has been considerable growth in the setting up of art fairs and markets for artists to sell their work. Almost every major town or city now has its own event. Many artists have found these events a very useful way of selling their work as they often attract a wide range of customers - from serious art collectors to the general public. They vary in type and quality; from the well-organised annual Art in the City held in Sheffield to the more informal weekly art market held on Sundays in Merrion Park, Dublin. Whatever the type of work you produce there will be an event suitable for your work.

How to find a fair

Your first point of contact for local fairs is the Arts Officer at the local council. Sometimes these people are known as Cultural Officers. Regional Arts Boards should also have details of fairs. Some events feature a particular type of work and others are broad-based. Some are restricted to dealers to take stands and others encourage individual artists to rent their own space.

Over the past few years some cities have developed art markets at which artists can rent a booth or space to display their work. Many of these are outdoors and have a very festive air.

Before choosing an event, do some research. Consider local venues first – remember that if you have to travel and stay overnight this will increase costs. Select events and venues which will complement the style of your work, consider the location, venue, quality of the organisation and the type of customers that it is likely to attract. Try and visit as many fairs and markets as possible. Ask other artists which fairs they consider to be the best, but remember that fairs may vary from year to year.

The cost of the stand should reflect the event's success. Cheap does not necessarily mean cost effective; you may be better paying more money for a better venue that suits your work.

Remember, with popular markets you might not be accepted the first time, and it may take time to obtain a good position. If there isn't one in your area, then why not try and organise one?

What to do at the event

Don't forget that most of the people who buy from art fairs will be collectors and may wish to purchase from you at another time. Hand out business cards or fliers with your details and information such as the type of work you make and whether you accept commissions.

You will need to leave the stand at times so either arrange for a friend to take over or ask the person on the next booth to look after your stand.

If the event is out of doors make sure that your work is

weatherproof, and take plenty of plastic sheeting. Always expect the worst and prepare accordingly. Arrive early to give yourself time to set up. Take a toolbox with everything you might need, including food!

Try and make the display attractive by balancing the size of the pieces. Try this out at home first. Clearly price all your work and have some method of wrapping the pieces. If they are very large, offer to deliver. If you exhibit at this type of event regularly it might be worth making arrangements to accept credit card payments, otherwise insist on cheque guarantee cards with cheques.

Be prepared to talk to people and keep a clipboard handy. Jot down names and addresses or ask for business cards so you can add them to your database. Don't apologise for your work: be confident. Start a conversation with, 'Do you like this type of work?' Most visitors will want to discuss the work, so be prepared for inane questions and remember this is the general public, not fellow artists.

Maximising the opportunity

If you have addresses of collectors or past customers in the area then don't forget to invite them along. If you've won any awards or had any publicity in the press, laminate the press cuttings and display them on your stand.

Follow up any enquiries after the fair; transfer the names and addresses onto your database. Record what happened, what you sold and how you could have improved your performance – you will have forgotten by the next time it comes round. Sometimes gallery owners visit this type of event looking for new artists, so keep some CVs and images handy.

At some events, painters may have to demonstrate. If you are not comfortable painting in public then avoid this type of event. Even if you are nervous of painting you could do some sketching, perhaps of the view or a still life. It's amazing how watching people work draws the crowds.

Selling by mail order

Selling direct to the public by mail shots or by advertising in magazines can be a very expensive but successful way of dealing directly with the customer. Originally used to supply overseas customers during the nineteenth century, it is still a very popular and effective way of promoting your business and products. For some craftworkers it works really well: for others, particularly those whose goods are not easily sent through the post, it can be a disaster.

The increased use of the Internet as a selling medium has expanded the marketplace, particularly for artists and printmakers, but the same basic principles apply. Its success depends on placing the advertisement in the right place and writing good copy for the advertisement.

The rules governing selling by mail order

This type of selling has suffered in the past from a poor public image as fraudulent advertisers frequently accepted the money and never supplied the goods. Consequently, industry regulation has been brought in to safeguard customers' interests. Most publications insist on safeguards for the public, and advertisers are expected to be able to supply the goods within 28 days.

In addition, all advertisements that ask for money in

advance must conform to the Mail Order Protection Scheme. Advertisers must declare to the scheme organisers the following information:

- Latest business accounts.
- A bank reference.
- Details of stock levels.
- Any advertising agents used.
- Details of the advertisement and product.

Additionally, all advertisements should conform to the Advertising Standards Code of Conduct. This does not apply to classified advertising.

Direct mail shots

Direct mail shots are an alternative to advertising in publications and can work well if you have your own customer base or access to good mailing lists. Types of mail shots include:

- Sending letters or leaflets through the post using a mailing list.
- Having leaflets delivered door to door.
- Leaving your leaflets in a variety of different locations to be picked up by the public. (This method is particularly popular for tourist attractions using hotels, tourist information centres, etc.)
- Putting an insert or flier in a trade or regional magazine.
- Having your leaflet included with other people's mail shots.

The effectiveness of direct mail shots

Direct mail is a powerful medium but one that is critically dependent on a sound mailing list and access to this may prove too expensive by far. Direct mail shots are very useful for selling to existing customers if you have built up your own database of their names and addresses.

What to sell

An advertisement can be specifically for one particular item or it can be for a range of items. Alternatively, a mail shot could contain copies of your catalogue or a flier with a special offer, a voucher for use in your shop, or anything else that you think will increase sales. Many craftworkers find that customers welcome a 'chatty' letter with an invitation to a craft fair where you are exhibiting or to an open day at your studio.

Selling from your home or studio

Selling your products directly to the customer is the most profitable option for many craftworkers and artists. How to achieve this can be a problem if you do not have your own studio from which you may retail. One solution is craft fairs but these do not always provide sufficient income or convenient venues. Another option is to take your goods directly to the customer. This type of selling is known as party plan. The original parties were held in people's houses, but nowadays parties can be held virtually anywhere: work canteens, village halls, or even a marquee in someone's garden.

Unless you are selling on a regular basis, it is unlikely

that you will need planning permission for party plan. A call to your local Planning Officer should tell you if there are any local bylaws that may affect your ability to trade. If you are selling from your home, you should also check your home insurance policy and mortgage agreement (or consult your landlord) as they may preclude any sort of commercial activity. If you intend to hold selling events on a regular basis at a public venue, you will almost certainly need to have a licence. The markets department at your local Town Hall usually issues these. Some authorities are stricter than others, so it's always wise to check.

The image of selling by party plan has improved since its first associations with plastic kitchenware. It is now one of the most successful methods of direct marketing and can be used to good advantage by craftworkers. Its many benefits include providing a captive audience, occupying a short period of time, having low overheads and the need to carry less stock. It can also provide customer feedback for those craftworkers who generally supply shops and galleries and do not deal directly with the customer.

If you are not skilled at selling then it is possible to employ someone to run the parties. One important point to think about is that the range of products on sale needs to be varied and interesting if it is to keep people entertained for a couple of hours, and you may need to consider combining your work with other craftworkers in order to provide variety.

How to get started

As with any business you need to plan ahead, work out the level of commission you can afford and prepare some printed price lists and order forms.

Most people begin by holding a party in their own or a friend's home. Organisations and charities also run these events in halls and other venues. You should aim to book at least one future party while at each party to ensure continuity.

You need a range of products with good profit margins, as party plan will not prove profitable if it comprises twenty guests and they all buy a £1.99 fridge magnet! This method of selling works particularly well when customers can collect things, like sets of pottery.

Incentives

You will need to work out how much you can afford to give the hostess, but it is generally between 10 and 20 per cent of your takings. Charities will want cash so you must take this into account. Some party planners give everyone a small free gift, a key-ring or something similar, and others find that playing a game with a small prize helps to break the ice.

Finance

The general feeling is that people will spend more if they order on the night and pay later. Ask everyone to fill in an order form – the hostess will need copies of these if she is to collect the money.

Arrange the delivery date at the party and ask the hostess to collect the money – do not leave goods unpaid for. If you cannot deliver any items, ring the customer and ask if he will accept an alternative. Always keep a note of all customers' names and addresses.

For a successful party, remember to:

- Make it entertaining – it is a social occasion.
- Offer incentives for booking parties.
- Include a re-order form with all orders.
- Keep a list of all customers and add to your database.
- Avoid school holidays.

Selling from your studio

An important factor in selling your work is having it seen by potential buyers. Once you have accumulated a saleable body of work you should start to look for a place to hold an exhibition. Your studio is obviously a good place to begin if it is accessible to the public. If your studio is small, cramped and in the back of beyond it is probably not a good place to hold an exhibition. Alternatively, if you or a friend live in a converted barn or other interesting property you might find holding an exhibition there will attract more people than a traditional gallery, as most people love to look round someone else's home.

If you are going to open your studio on a regular basis you need to advertise this fact and try to keep to regular times, for example, every Sunday afternoon. Some artists open their studios twice a year for the four weeks before Christmas and in the summer to encourage tourists. You will need to publicise the fact that you are open, mail out any customers you already have and place adverts in the local press. A notice in the studio window or on the door is also useful but often forgotten. Some towns have regular open studios when all the artists in the area open. These are usually very successful so if you have the opportunity to join one it's likely to be worthwhile.

Commissions

A public art project can be a very exciting thing to work on; it can develop creativity and inspire new ideas. You need to take your work out of the studio and into the world. Some artists do not like to work to commission as they feel it inhibits them, but it is possible to use your abilities without sacrificing your artistic integrity. Sculptors often find commissions a useful source of income, as do artists who work on murals.

To find a commission you should look at advertisements in arts magazines, such as *The Artist's Newsletter*. Sometimes a small number of people are invited to apply for a commission and in this case a fee is usually paid for your preparation. Beware of open competitions where you may need to do a lot of work and, in the end, have no reward.

Corporate commissions

Supplying art for businesses to furnish offices or to give as gifts can be very lucrative. Most of this work comes via the various slide indexes at the Crafts Council and Arts Boards. You can also approach companies directly if you have a specific suggestion for work; for example, if you work in concrete then you could approach a concrete manufacturer with a CV and photographs of your work. Just make sure it's a specific proposal.

Always make sure that you get maximum publicity from any commission as this may lead to further commissions.

Chapter 9:

Pricing Your Work

One of the dilemmas faced when starting a creative business is how to price work. It is a difficult question to answer, as each business is different. There are, however, general guidelines which can be applied to any business, although there are differences in the way original art work like paintings and sculpture are priced compared to production work.

Pricing craftwork

The first thing you have to calculate is how much the product costs you to make. Unless you are covering your costs then every time you sell a product you are literally giving money away. Experience has shown that basing your prices on what the craftworker on the next stall is charging, without calculating your costs, is the sure way to disaster.

The joke about the craftworker who won the lottery and, when asked what he would do with the money, replied, "Keep doing the craft fairs until the money runs out," unfortunately has a ring of truth about it! The people who are prepared to work for little or no return do no favours to themselves or to other craftworkers. Setting unrealistic prices simply stops the industry from developing.

To calculate the prices you should charge, you need to calculate the costs involved. These fall into three categories: production costs, overheads and selling costs. To these will need to be added a profit margin.

Production costs

These are the easiest costs to calculate. It will probably be easier to calculate the costs for a batch of products rather than trying to work out an individual cost, unless you work to commission, in which case each piece of work will have to be calculated separately. Production costs cover two main areas: the materials used and the labour costs.

1. MATERIALS

To calculate the cost of materials simply charge to each object the cost of the raw materials required to make it. Depending on your craft, you may also need to allow for wastage.

2. LABOUR

The easiest way to calculate an hourly labour cost is to decide how much you would hope to earn in a year, divide this figure by, say, 48 weeks and then by the number of hours, say, 40. When deciding how much you need to earn, do work out your needs properly. Rent, council tax, food, services, etc., all need to be included, and add some money on for contingency and holidays – even craftworkers need a break. The resulting hourly rate should then be appropriate even if you only actually work part-time, perhaps during the school term.

Overheads

These include all the costs involved in running your business and workshop, which have to be paid whether you are working or not. Working out the overheads becomes easier after you have been in business for a year or more as you can base your calculations on last year's figures. However, it needs to be done from the beginning, so have a go. Overheads also need to be calculated on an annual basis. They can be divided into four headings:

1. WORKSHOP EXPENSES

These include rent, mortgage repayments, rates, electricity, gas, maintenance and repairs. If you are working from home then you should estimate a percentage of your household bills and include that figure. For example, if you will mostly use one main room out of five such rooms in your house, your percentage might reasonably be evaluated as 20 per cent.

2. BUSINESS EXPENSES

These include telephone, postage, travelling and car costs, insurance and professional fees, such as those of your accountant.

3. EQUIPMENT AND LOANS

You may have borrowed money to start a business and need to include the repayment costs. If you use expensive equipment, which may have to be replaced, allow a percentage of the replacement cost calculated by your assessment of the expected life of the equipment. This should then be 'saved' so you can afford to replace the equipment when it becomes necessary. As your business grows you may also need to purchase new equipment.

4. STOCK

Stocks of raw materials or products which are just sitting on a shelf are costing you money. Calculate 20 per cent of the average stock value and add to the overheads.

When you have calculated all your overheads on a full year basis, divide the figure by the full-time number of weeks and then hours that you might expect to work. This will give you an hourly overhead rate, which can be used with the hourly labour rate, whether or not you work full-time.

Selling costs

These should include craft fair fees, advertising costs, photography, production of publicity material, agent's fees or commission, shelf rental etc. If you need to stay overnight when you go to fairs these costs should either be added in here or as business expenses. Many craftworkers find it difficult, particularly in the early stages, to work out the selling costs. If this is your problem, add a fixed percentage, say 20 per cent of the production and overhead costs, as in the example on page 94.

Profit margin

When you have calculated the costs involved in producing your work you need to add a profit margin to cover breakages, unexpected bills and so on.

Using the cost price to calculate the selling price

Once you have calculated your cost price you can then decide the selling price. This will be influenced by where you sell the products and what your competitors charge. The actual mark-up may vary from piece to piece. Some of your lines may prove to be more profitable than others, and obviously these are the ones of which you wish to produce more. If you sell to shops and at craft fairs you may have either to produce different ranges for each market or increase your craft fair prices in line with the retailers.

VAT

If you are registered for VAT, you must add VAT to all sales.

Commissions

Costing for commissions involves the same basic process, except that you will be costing in advance and estimating the time and materials. This obviously becomes easier with experience, but be careful as expensive mistakes can be made. Overestimate rather than undercharge and don't forget to allow for design time.

Example

There are various approaches to costing and in larger businesses costing can be very complicated. However, for a small craftworker it is best to use a simple method, such as the one set out overleaf which can be adapted for your needs.

The following costing method is designed for craftworkers who are working full-time. If you share premises or only work part-time then you will need to adjust the figures.

A craftworker produces 20 jugs a day. To calculate the individual cost of each jug first calculate the cost of the batch.

Production costs	Materials	£20.00
	Labour (8 hours @ £10 per hour)	£80.00
Overheads	£1 per hour	£8.00
Subtotal		**£108.00**
Selling costs	20%	£21.60
Total cost for 20 jugs		£129.60
Cost per jug		**£6.48**
Profit margin	20%	£1.30
TOTAL		**£7.78**

The selling price of the jug needs to be at least £7.78. This basic price can then be increased in relation to the region in which it is being sold and what the competition is charging for similar products.

Remember

- You may not sell every item that you make.
- If the process you use has quality problems you will need to allow for this.
- If you are going to sell to shops and at fairs you will need to ensure that the selling price at both is comparable.

- You are more likely to succeed profitably by selling goods yourself since retailers need to add often substantial mark-ups to cover their overheads.

Pricing artwork

Pricing is one of the most difficult tasks facing the artist when starting out. Most prices of artwork are related to the prices paid for work sold recently but, until you have sold something, you don't really know how much people will pay for your work. Price too cheaply and you risk undervaluing your work; put your prices too high and you risk not selling anything.

There are four criteria to be used when pricing art:

1. AESTHETIC AND TECHNICAL MERITS

This is the level of skill involved in making the artwork and the training you have undertaken. The 60-year-old artist who says that it has taken him 40 years to paint a picture is saying that 40 years' experience and practice have gone into that work.

2. THE COSTS AND TIME ASSOCIATED WITH PRODUCING THE WORK

These overhead costs will include a proportion of expenses such as studio rent, insurance, electricity, and materials.

3. MARKETING COSTS

This includes costs in staging an exhibition, having leaflets printed and so on.

4. YOUR REPUTATION OR PREVIOUS PRICES
An artist who sells his pictures as fast as he can paint them should be able gradually to keep increasing prices.

The price cannot be determined solely by the time and materials invested in it. However, it is useful to know how long a piece takes you and how many saleable pieces you make in a given period. This is essential if you are to make a living at your work.

In addition to the above criteria, there are times when some artwork suddenly commands a higher price due to the demands of fashion and economic factors. Work that starts to be bought by collectors can suddenly increase an artist's value. So finding out where to position your work involves taking into account all these factors.

Research

If you are just starting out, you need to research the market, visit shows and exhibitions, and find out how much other people charge for their work. Pay particular attention to new artists who will not have been able to include any value for reputation. Prices also vary according to area: London galleries are able to command higher prices than those in the provinces.

Try and assess objectively if your work is better than theirs, or is more saleable, and charge accordingly. Don't forget that the price shown is not the one that the artists receive, as there will almost certainly be a commission to be paid.

When you begin to sell regularly you can start to increase your prices gradually. You will need to remain competitive within the marketplace in order to carry on selling. Take advantage of anything which increases your reputation, such as winning a competition. If there is a particular piece that you do not want to part with, then it's fine to charge more. If you think a painting might sell well as prints, then set this up before selling the original.

Don't undervalue your work. If you don't value it fully then no-one else will; but, by the same token, don't try and sell everything - just your best work - or your reputation will suffer.

Price list

Establish a price list and do not deviate from it. If a piece is worth £200 in a gallery then it is worth £200 in your studio. People who are regular customers or who buy more than one painting from you can be offered a discount, but you cannot expect galleries to support you and display your work if they know that you are undercutting them.

Always make sure that the customer knows exactly what is included in the sale. If you charge extra for credit card sales, framing, shipping and hanging, then you must say so.

Don't ever sell anything that you are not prepared to sign and have recognised as your work. If you demonstrate and find that people ask to buy your demonstration pieces, only sell them if you would do so normally; they may get in the wrong hands and have an adverse effect on your reputation in years to come. Although you should be proud of everything you sell, you should price your best work higher and, if you produce an exceptionally good piece, consider entering it in a prestigious exhibition, rather than just selling it.

At the end of the day, the price you receive for your work is the price that someone is prepared to pay.

Questions often asked about pricing fine art

DO OIL PAINTINGS FETCH HIGHER PRICES THAN ACRYLICS?
Generally speaking, an oil painting will command a higher price than either a watercolour or acrylic by the same artist if they are comparable in size and subject matter.

DO WORKS BY MALE ARTISTS SELL FOR MORE THAN BY FEMALE ARTISTS?
Female artists still maintain that they have a more difficult time than men in getting their work exhibited and receiving a good price. Some women deliberately sign their work so it is impossible to tell whether they are male or female, but this can be counterproductive if you are trying to build a reputation.

IF I AM HAVING AN EXHIBITION, WILL THE GALLERY OWNER SET THE PRICES?
No. A gallery owner will ask you how much you expect for a piece and then discuss this with you but he will expect you to know how much you think your work is worth.

ARE PRICES THE SAME ALL OVER THE COUNTRY?
The market for works of art is strongest in the South East and therefore the prices tend to be higher. Galleries in very expensive areas may charge a higher commission in order to cover their overheads.

Chapter 10:
Marketing

Promoting yourself

To further your career, it is essential that you develop the art of self-promotion. The more effort and time you spend on promoting yourself, the better your chances of success. Whether we like it or not, being an artist today does mean being involved in the business side of art. There are a lot of talented artists in the field, but there are not a lot of active artists and it is these who make a living by spending as much time promoting their work as they do creating.

To promote yourself properly you must have the right attitude. You have to believe in your work and to make a positive commitment to its worth. You have to believe that people not only need but also want art, and you can provide for this need by doing something you love. There really is no need to struggle along, starving in a garret in the traditional fashion.

You must have a commitment not only to producing the work but to selling it as well. You will need a certain level of discipline, particularly if you have to do other work to pay the bills in the meantime. A gallery owner says that most of the successful artists he knows spend at least 50 hours a week actually creating work. Another successful artist says that she averages 20 hours a week painting and 25 hours a week promoting her work. This type of work-load is a heavy commitment and, if you are not prepared to make it, then do you really want to sell your work?

Market research

Before you start producing in quantity and investing money in your work, you should do some market research to find out if people will buy your product. If you make wearable items, this can be as simple as wearing them everywhere and taking notes of the comments people make. If people ask you where you bought something it is always a good sign. You can also ask friends and family for comments, but these are not always very objective. If you regularly attend craft fairs then you will automatically receive feedback from the customers. Similarly, if you are an artist try and attend your own exhibition incognito and listen to the comments, or ask the gallery owner for feed-back. Some preliminary market research can save you making some very expensive mistakes!

Potential markets

Make a list of potential markets for your products. Depending on the type of work, these could include trade customers such as:

- Book stores.
- Churches.
- Country clubs.
- Department stores.
- Galleries.

- Gift shops.
- Home exhibitions.
- Hotels.
- Interior designers.
- Museums.
- Restaurants.
- Speciality markets.
- Slide registries.

It could also include individuals such as:

- Academics.
- Architects.
- Art publishers.
- Book publishers.
- Businessmen.
- Collectors.
- Corporations.
- Tourists.

Presenting a positive image

Image is just as important to small businesses as to large ones. The image is the strongest factor in influencing the customer's perceptions of the business. It will reflect the quality of your products or services, the attitude of your staff, and your level of efficiency. The image is, in effect, the human face of the business. A positive image makes the difference between failure and success.

Every time you contact your customers the message they receive will influence the way they think about you. Whether it's at a craft fair or over the telephone, subconsciously people will give you a character, and this often determines why someone buys one person's work rather than another's. Customers will prefer certain businesses because they are made to feel important.

Many craftworkers consider that their image is their stationery and look no further than the printed word. This is a mistake - the image should run through the whole business.

Obtaining the right image need not be expensive but it does require a lot of thought, particularly in the initial stages. If you employ professionals, such as a graphic designer, they should insist on meeting you and talking to you about your business and the type of customers you intend to serve. Be very wary of printers who say they have an artist available as they may just feed you a logo off a computer package and you could find you are using the same logo as a number of other companies. If you require a logo and cannot afford to employ a graphic designer, you might find an art student or a fellow craft worker willing to supply a few samples for a modest fee.

The image of a business aiming at the top end of the gallery market will be entirely different from that of a business trading mainly through local craft fairs. Both businesses may well be extremely profitable, but for different reasons. When planning your image it is essential that you know to which market you are aiming. Refer back to the customer profile you created, as described on page 66.

The name of the business

If you are starting a business, consider its name very carefully. A trading name that reflects exactly the required image can be an enormous advantage when setting up. It should be easy to remember and should trip off the tongue easily. Options include:

- Using your own name, e.g. 'Jane Birch Ceramics'.
- Using the name of a local town, river or county, e.g. 'The Anyshire Ceramics Co'.
- Using a descriptive name, such as 'Ceramic Cats'.
- Using something catchy or amusing, e.g. 'Crazy Cats'.

If you have trouble deciding on a name, hold a brainstorming session with family, friends or colleagues. Write down all the possible titles you can think of, and list associated words using a thesaurus. Choose six possibilities and check in the local telephone and craftworkers' directories that there isn't another business with a similar name. Ask your friends to consider the remaining titles and the image they project.

House colours

Choice of colour for your publicity material is very important as colours trigger people's perceptions. Every colour portrays a different image. Dark colours tend to be smarter and more traditional. Deep green, burgundy and navy blue are often used by upmarket retailers to purvey quality. Yellows are cheerful and fun and can be introduced as a second colour to promote a more modern image. Red is the best-selling colour for some products, but some shades can convey cheapness. Green and brown give a rustic, homespun impression. Brown used alone can be very dull, however. Put gold with dark green for an upmarket image.

Different shades of the same colour can give different images. Mid-tone greens are good for interiors and environmental products. Pastel shades are generally considered feminine and unprofessional but can therefore be ideal for lingerie.

If you intend to export your goods, check that the colours you choose do not convey any adverse message to another country. For instance, white means death in Japan.

Lettering style

Find a style that suits your craftwork and fits in with the rest of your image. This style should be continued throughout all of your marketing and billing paperwork.

Promotional material

Do your customers know who you are, what you make or where you are? Unless you tell them, they may never find out. You will need a range of promotional material to suit different occasions. Every business needs stationery and business cards; you will also need fliers, price lists and possibly a brochure or catalogue. If you are going for commissions then you will also need a portfolio. Your promotional material should reflect your image and help you create an identity which will be easily recognised by your customers.

Promotional material includes, as appropriate: advertisements, brochures, business cards, fliers, letterheads, logos, photos of yourself, photos of your work, portfolio postcards, press releases and slides or transparencies.

Logos

A logo is important, as it is something people can focus on and remember. It could simply be your signature, or it could be something specially designed to reflect your craft. Some of the best logos arrive by accident, so try doodling and see what the results are like. An eye-catching logo can make a great first impression. Keep your logo to one or two colours to keep costs down. If it will need to be reproduced scaled down in size, make sure that it will still be clear. Spend as much time and effort on your logo as you do on your product, because that is what it will come to represent.

Stationery

Almost the first thing a new business orders is a range of stationery. Sometimes, in the hectic build-up to a new business, there isn't a lot of thought given to the style and design of the stationery. Later on in the life of the business, even when there is more time, few people review their stationery; they simply re-order the same again because that is easier. However, you will find that few successful businesses are still using the same logo, colours and font that they were five years ago. You need to remain vigilant. The public's perceptions change and, in our fast moving society, a business can quickly become old-fashioned. If you cannot design your own stationery, find a graphic designer. Do not leave it to the printers, as they are not generally known for their artistic skills.

Essential business stationery includes:

Business cards

These should show the company name and logo, your name, qualifications (if applicable), address, telephone and fax numbers, e-mail and website addresses. There are many different card styles to choose from, so shop around to find something that fits your company's image. Cards can be laminated, reflective, embossed and they can also carry a photograph. They can be printed on a wide range of paper, plastic or card.

Letterheads

These can be used not only for letters but also for invoices, statements and receipts. They should feature all the necessary information such as name of business, address and contact details. If you are not using your name for the business then it is a good idea to include that as well. If you are registered for VAT then include your registration number.

Brochures

Producing a brochure that describes your craftwork is a good idea; it is essential if you are selling to the trade. The brochure doesn't need to be very elaborate if you do not have the funding. Colour photographs are important; you may be able to scan these into a computer.

The brochure could include descriptions of your work, details of your artistic philosophy and perhaps testimonials from satisfied customers or persons of note in your field.

You may want to obtain professional advice; however, you should have the 'final say' on matters such as cover and back page design; typestyle; layout; colour and type of paper; graphics and, importantly, your logo. Think carefully before deciding how many to have printed – you may find it more economical to print in bulk, but bear in mind that you may want to change the brochure annually, or even quarterly, and so will not want to be left with too many surplus.

As a general rule brochures should:

- Be written in simple English, avoiding technical jargon.
- Be illustrated.
- Not be more than four A5 or A4 pages long.
- Not contain prices - these should be on a separate leaflet, as they will date quickly.

Postcards

These can be produced from photographs, slides and from artwork. They are an excellent way of promoting your craft and many craftworkers sell them to customers as well.

Address labels

Every time you send out a product or information sheet do ensure that your name and address are clearly displayed. The cheapest and easiest way to do this is using sticky labels. They come on rolls and are a very cheap way of identifying photographs etc.

Setting objectives

In the same way as you set objectives for your business, you should also set them for your reputation. You need to set goals, such as winning awards, getting your name in print, or being selected for exhibitions. In order to establish your reputation, your first objectives should be to write a good CV, compile an excellent portfolio and to use them to enter for commissions and exhibitions.

Writing a CV

A CV for a craftworker is slightly different from the traditional one that most people use when applying for jobs. It needs to be very focused and to contain details of the type of work you have done, and possibly a statement of your artistic philosophy. The CV should really be kept on computer and updated constantly so that it is applicable to whatever you are applying for. A CV will be required by all galleries when applying for an exhibition and also for funding applications.

As a general rule a CV should be no longer than two sides of A4 paper. In exceptional circumstances, such as when applying for an international award where it is important that all your experience is included, the CV could be longer.

It is always a good idea to include a postcard or photograph of your work, clearly labelled on the back. If you are applying for television work, or another position where your appearance is important, then a personal photograph can also be included.

Suggested layout

NAME:	Give your first name before your surname, e.g. Janet Brown.
ADDRESS:	Give your full home address and include the postcode.

STUDIO ADDRESS:	Give your studio address or current work address. (If you work from home then leave this section out.)
TELEPHONE:	Give your telephone number during the day if possible, as well as home and mobile numbers. You may also want to include your e-mail and website addresses, if you have these.
DATE OF BIRTH/AGE:	If you give your age, remember to update it every year!
EDUCATION:	Give relevant details of schools, colleges and universities attended and qualifications gained.
SPECIALIST TRAINING:	Any courses you have undertaken relating to your work.
WORK EXPERIENCE:	List all relevant work experience.
EXHIBITIONS:	Include attendance at major events, e.g. Chelsea Craft Fair.
VOLUNTARY WORK:	Give details of activities such as acting as Secretary of a local craft guild or membership of a charity.
LEISURE INTERESTS:	Give details of one or two hobbies which may or may not be art related.
REFEREES:	Include the names and addresses of at least two people who are willing to act as referees. At least one should be a former employer. Always check that they are prepared to act in this way.

Compiling a portfolio

For people working as illustrators, or fine artists, a good portfolio is essential. Be selective, make sure its contents are focused on the opportunity in hand and keep it current.

A general portfolio could include:

- Twenty high quality images of your most current work. These should be easily viewed.
- Prints can be effective, as the impression is immediate. If your work is three dimensional then include photographs from different angles. Do not include any original work.
- Photocopies of publicity from newspapers and magazines.
- A CV or personal statement.
- A photograph of yourself (optional).

A portfolio may be used:

- To get into a gallery.
- To show a prospective representative.
- To obtain a job interview.
- To apply for a grant.
- To obtain a commission.

If applying for a commission, competition, or residency, always be careful to follow any instructions given by the company or organiser. Adjust your portfolio for each application – try and find out what the recipient wants to see. Some galleries prefer slides; others prefer photographs. Presentation is almost as important as content – make sure all your work is clean, tidy and labelled.

Display

Crafts are a visual medium and displaying them properly is a vital part of your marketing strategy. Whether it is in your studio, at a craft fair or in an exhibition, every opportunity must be taken to present your products in the best possible light to maximise the potential sales. This doesn't mean that you have to spend a lot of money on expensive equipment. It is amazing what can be done with a little ingenuity. The exception to this is when exhibiting at a trade fair. Professional presentation is very important and if you are not able to design and build a stand of suitable quality then you will need help.

Craft fairs

When exhibiting alongside other craftworkers, a professional display will attract people to your stand and improve business. Before you go, try and find out what space you will have, particularly if there is any wall space. At some craft fairs you will be limited to a table space and you will only be able to stand behind this. If this is the case, the table should be completely covered to hide any boxes or packing underneath. To present an attractive image, try and colour co-ordinate everything. All the display stands and fabric used should match. If your products are very colourful then go for a neutral colour, like cream or black. Sometimes a bright background lifts the products, so experiment with different fabrics. To create areas of interest try and make sure you add some height to your display. If you intend to exhibit regularly at craft fairs then design a stand which is flexible, as you might not always have the same size space.

Trade fairs

At a trade fair you will simply be supplied with a 'shell' and power points, as ordered. You then have the opportunity to create either a walk-in area, if the space is big enough, or use it for a professionally designed stand. Again, consider how you can display your crafts to their best advantage and don't forget to consider security. Retailers like to see how the goods can be displayed in their shop, so think about this when you plan your displays. If you produce special display stands for your products, then your trade customers might be interested in purchasing/borrowing these as well as your crafts. You could offer a package deal.

Improvising display material

Start by considering your own goods - can any of them be used as display items? Look around the home: mug trees can be used for jewellery, clotheshorses for scarves or clothes. Visit the garden centre and see what they have on offer - trellis can be used in many ways if painted to match your business colours. Cover sturdy boxes with fabric or paper in your colours. Use plant pots and pine shelves to build a display. The possibilities are endless and a little imagination can easily produce whatever best suits your needs. If you sell cards, don't try and improvise with these as good display is essential. A spinner will almost always increase sales. Second-hand spinners are often advertised in papers such as *Loot* under 'shop fitters', or you could try asking at card shops away from your district, making it clear that you are not going to compete with them.

Commercial display products

When you begin in crafts, spending money on display items may seem to be extravagant. In fact, it is vital. A professional display promotes the added value of your goods. *The Craftsman* magazine carries advertisements for suppliers of display material and packaging which are tailored to craftworkers' needs. Alternatively, most large towns have a shop fitting store that may stock stands that you can use. The address will be in the *Yellow Pages.*

Lighting

When designing your stand, don't forget about the lighting. Would you buy from a shop window that was dark and gloomy? Chain store spotlights can often be utilised to keep costs down, or you could visit factory lighting shops. Check how many plug points will be available before you begin to plan your display.

Point of sale material

A good display will always contain some point of sale material. Photographs of your studio and products can enhance a display and draw customers to your stand. A flier with details of your history, training and motivation, along with other details of where your work is available, is useful. Don't forget a price list and/or order form with a sketch of the product to remind people about your work. You may want to laminate some point of sale material to make it look more professional. Shops and galleries may require photographs and more upmarket material.

Custom-built display stands

If you can afford it, consider having a specially designed stand. These can be made so that they fold away easily and are a boon if you are exhibiting every weekend. You may be able to design something yourself and find a local joiner who will build you a portable stand to your design. Remember that it will need to fit in your car or van and, if you exhibit alone, you will need to be able to transport it easily. Look around at your competitors and see what works for them and then decide if it will work for you. Good ideas can always be adapted.

Pricing

Don't forget to price your products clearly and professionally. At a trade show you may prefer to have a separate price list, but do make sure that it is easily available. If you are offering any special deals then make sure people are aware of them.

Chapter 11:

Supplying the Trade

Most craft workers gain their initial experience of selling by exhibiting at craft fairs or by selling from their studio. For some, especially those who enjoy the lifestyle of the craft fair circuit, this provides sufficient income and a market for all their production. For others who want to expand their business and enjoy the experience of seeing their work sold in retail outlets, exhibiting at a trade show can be the most cost-effective way of reaching trade customers.

Opportunities to exhibit at trade fairs have never been greater: there are an ever-increasing number of fairs both in the UK and in Europe. However, before you embark on this route, you need to ask yourself the following questions:

1. Do you have the financial capacity to handle increased sales? Trade customers will want credit and, if you are under-capitalised and receive a lot of orders, you could end up with cash flow problems.
2. What are your production levels? Can you produce enough extra stock to warrant the cost of taking a stand? Can you deliver the goods on time?
3. Will your suppliers be able to meet the increased demand for raw materials?

4. Do you have the space to hold the extra stock necessary?
5. Can you 'sell' your work to trade buyers? This needs a different marketing approach from craft fairs.
6. Will your work travel, and will the cost of carriage be prohibitive?

Do your research

Having decided that you have the ability to exhibit at trade fairs, the next step is to identify which show is right for you. If possible, always visit the show before you exhibit. Talk to the other exhibitors and the organisers so you can make a good start. You will need to decide whether you are going to exhibit alone or with a group. In the case of some of the bigger fairs which have waiting lists, the only way you can exhibit is by joining a group stand. The best of these judge the products to ensure a consistently high standard, which does attract the buyers. If you are on a Prince's Trust scheme or belong to a marketing organisation you may be able to get financial support to exhibit.

Selecting a show

Your choice of show will depend on availability and on what you want to achieve. If you are looking for export orders then you may choose one fair; if you are looking for department stores, you may choose another. Some shows offer packages or special discounts for new exhibitors. Contact the organisers of the shows in which you are interested and ask for an exhibitor's pack. The pack should provide you with the following information:

1. Customers. The number and type of buyers, and whether they are from multiples, gallery owners, or overseas. Are the people who go to their shops your potential customers?
2. Awards. Are there any awards, which could be turned into opportunities for promotion?
3. Reputation. How long has the show been going? Which organisation sponsors the show?
4. Cost. What do the costs include? Are electricity and lighting included in the package? Are tables, chairs and shelving included? (When budgeting, don't forget to include travel and accommodation costs.)
5. Restrictions. What can you exhibit? Are there limits on the heights of the stands, the number of personnel, use of models or demonstrations or music?
6. Timing. Does the show fit into your schedule or does it compete with other shows? If you are going to be taking Christmas orders, will it give you enough time to produce them?

The shows

Trade shows change from year to year as new halls are added, or the product emphasis is changed. Check out the current state of the fairs below:

The British Craft Trade Fair (Harrogate)

The UK's only specialist trade fair is held each year in Harrogate. It provides a good starting point and attracts mainly gallery and independent buyers. They offer a special deal for newcomers, which is a cost-effective way to test the market.

The Spring Fair (Birmingham)

Billed as the largest gift fair in Europe, the only way for a newcomer to exhibit here will probably be on a group stand or to join a long waiting list. With such a large fair it is important to be in the right place or the buyers will miss you. It is now divided into specialist sections, which may or may not work to your advantage, depending on the type of work you produce.

The Autumn Fair (Birmingham)

This, the younger of the Trade Promotions Services fairs, is well placed for orders for the profitable Christmas period, so long as you can meet the demand. It has made an effort to attract design-led exhibitors in recent years.

Top Drawer (London)

This fair is held three times a year in the spring, summer and autumn. These shows have large design-led sections and attract a lot of export buyers.

Other fairs include *The Glasgow Trade Fair*, *The Highland Gift Fair*, *The Welsh Craft Fair*, *The West Country Gift Fair*, *The Llandudno Gift Fair* and *Cumbrex*.

There are a number of smaller regional fairs, but these are mainly staffed by agents of large manufacturers. If you attract a large number of buyers in one area, a regional fair may be useful for maintaining contact.

Booking space

Some spaces are definitely better than other, but, as most shows book space on a seniority system, it may be a while before you get one, and you may have to take what is available in the first year. Once you have started exhibiting, don't be afraid to ask for a better position. You can compensate to some extent for a poor position by making the best use of the space and inviting as many buyers as possible to the show. If you make the right choice in the first place and stay for a few years then you should get a good pitch.

Group stands

For craftworkers who are starting out, an increasingly popular option is the group stand. There are two types of group stand. The first is where a large organiser, such as *Focal Point* or *Design Gap*, rents a space at the exhibition and then sublets it to small businesses. These organisations will usually want to see your work before they accept you. The second is where an organisation or group of people rent a stand, which then contains several people's work. They usually operate a rota system for manning the stand but some people find it hard to sell other people's crafts.

How to have a successful show

You can have a significant impact on the success of your show by taking a professional approach.

12 Golden Rules

1. Read the exhibitor's handbook thoroughly and make sure that you have ordered everything you need.

2. Rent one of the Video Arts training videos on successful exhibiting.
3. Arrive at the show on time, allowing as long as possible to erect your stand, since reaching the hall itself can take ages at some fairs.
4. Organise reliable helpers for the fair and make sure that they are fully briefed on your business. It is not acceptable at a trade show to ask 'next door' to keep an eye on your stand. You may also have a considerable distance to transport your goods, so bear this in mind when deciding how many 'hands' you will need.
5. Make sure that you not only have that vital order book on your stand but also a book for potential leads and business cards. Have a system by which you can check your 'running stock position' as you take orders, and possibly suggest delivery dates.
6. Start designing your stand as soon as possible and have a trial run. Remember that trade buyers will wonder how your products will look in their shops, so pay particular attention to your display which needs to be as interesting as possible and feature point of sale display material.
7. Don't build a barrier between you and your customers. They should be able to get on your stand easily.
8. Highlight new products and any awards. The words 'new' and 'success' are very powerful, so use them in your publicity.
9. It is unlikely that you can demonstrate at a trade fair but you can have photographs of yourself in your studio.
10. If posters and photographs can enhance your exhibits then use large ones and make sure that they are professionally produced.

11. Offer a special deal, available only at the show, to encourage buyers.
12. Don't worry too much if you don't achieve the orders you expected - buyers often like time to consider new products, and sometimes you may have to wait until the second year.

Follow up

After the show, contact all the buyers who left their card. Following up the leads from a show can often be the most important part of exhibiting.

Trade fairs for artists

Some artists, particularly those who sell prints and cards, or who are looking to supply their work to the large manufacturers, exhibit at the spring and autumn shows and everything above applies to them. Most artists sell through galleries and there is quite a reasonable trade between galleries. *The Battersea Art Fair* and *The London Art Fair* are the main showcases, but it is generally galleries who exhibit at these, rather than individual artists.

Trade fairs for designers

There are several major shows for designers in London, the two most popular being *100% Design* and *Mode*. There are selection procedures for these shows. Visit them to see if they would be useful for you.

Chapter 12:

Galleries and Exhibitions

Approaching galleries and arranging exhibitions of your work is not as difficult as it may first appear. Sometimes people refuse offers of exhibitions because they are not sure what is expected of them and whether they can cope, but it can be a very rewarding and exciting experience.

Exhibitions can either be the work of one craftworker or a group. Sometimes the combination of work by two makers such as a fine artist and ceramicist can be to the benefit of both of them. It is important to decide exactly why you want an exhibition. Is it to sell your work, obtain commissions or to raise your profile?

There are five main reasons for exhibiting your work:

1. To show your work to the public. Most craftworkers value this contact with a wider audience.
2. To give you the opportunity to see your work displayed in its entirety, in good, well lit surroundings which show it off to its best perspective.
3. To establish your reputation as a craftworker, and to introduce yourself to fellow craftworkers, other exhibition organisers, galleries and collectors.
4. To sell your work and obtain commissions. You will obviously need to cover the costs of preparing the exhibition and bring in income.

5. To provide a focus for your working life. Having an exhibition can be wonderfully motivating.

Possible venues

There are a surprising number of places prepared to exhibit work. Some offer their facilities free and others charge or take a commission. Always remember that you put a lot of work into an exhibition and you want as many people as possible to see it, so a good location is the main priority. Sometimes you can find places to exhibit your work where it is not possible to sell. Don't dismiss these out of hand – they might lead to increased business, provided the work is clearly identified and people can contact you easily. Craftworkers at Manchester Craft and Design Centre have noticed an increase in the number of visitors since their work was on display at Manchester Airport, not a traditional place for craftworkers to exhibit. Some venues put restrictions on the type of work displayed. For example, some charitable organisations will not display items which they consider to be against their aims.

The following list of venues should give you some idea of the types of places available.

Studio exhibitions

When finding a venue to exhibit your work look first at what you have available yourself. You will need to check if you require any type of planning permission, but it is unlikely to be necessary for a short-term exhibition.

Building society or bank windows

Window space on a high street can be very valuable and any sort of business that does not serve the retail trade may make its windows available. It may help if you are an existing customer of the business, otherwise try and fit in with a local festival or Christmas, when organisations may be looking for a way of decorating their windows.

Local authority galleries

Many local authorities and some of the smaller tourist attractions have gallery space at reasonable prices, although this often gets booked-up well in advance. Enterprise Agencies and business organisations may have display space for local work or will use your work to decorate a stand at an exhibition. They often find it difficult to find attractive products made locally, particularly in areas where heavy industry or service industries predominate, so it is always worth making them aware of your work. This can also lead to corporate commissions.

Private galleries

Private or commercial galleries are the most commonly used venues for exhibitions. You will need to check with the owners regarding their policy on exhibitions. They generally like to nurture craftworkers and artists they feel have potential but sometimes have specialist exhibitions where they exhibit work by a variety of craftworkers and you may be able to be included in this type of exhibition.

Showcases

Showcases are available in large hotels and corporate buildings. They can prove a useful place for exposure, particularly if you work to commission rather than selling individual items.

Foyers

Foyers of theatres, concert halls, cinemas and so on are increasingly being used for this type of event to provide an added attraction for their patrons.

Libraries and Tourist Information Centres

Libraries and Tourist Information Centres often have a room which is used for exhibitions. The cost is usually more reasonable than that charged by the commercial galleries but you may be surprised by the results as these venues attract a wide variety of people.

Approaching a gallery

It is generally a waste of time trying to persuade someone to exhibit work totally different from their usual format, so look for galleries who often exhibit similar work to yours. Your local Arts Council may have details of exhibition space. Most local authorities now have Arts Officers who may offer assistance, and you should look at advertisements in newspapers for other exhibitions to identify potential venues. Remember that popular venues get booked up well in advance, sometimes two or three years ahead. You could always ask if there is anyone with an exhibition already booked who may be willing to share the exhibition. If you are trying to exhibit in a local shop window, approach the manager and be prepared to leave samples of your work and publicity material, as he may have to check with head office.

Working out a budget

The cost of holding an exhibition should not be underestimated and this may be why it is often sensible initially to share an exhibition with others. Before you agree to an exhibition sit down and work out the costs. These will include:

- *Hire of venue*. In some cases there may be a fixed charge or the gallery could accept a percentage. However, this will usually require a guaranteed minimum payment. Find out what the hire of the venue includes – sometimes the gallery will be responsible for the cost of the private view, at other times you will be responsible for everything.
- *Catalogue printing*. All exhibitions need a catalogue and these can be very expensive to produce. However, with the increasing sophistication of computers, you may be able to do this yourself. If your work needs a fully illustrated catalogue this may be expensive but you may be able to recover some of the costs by selling them. Colour postcards of your main pieces, accompanied by a printed price list, may be an alternative to a traditional catalogue, and these are particularly useful if you plan to rotate the pieces on display.
- *Posters*. If you are trying to attract the general public to your show then you may need to print some

posters. If your work is particularly collectable you may be able to sell the posters at the exhibition to try and recover some of the cost.

- *Publicity*. The amount you need to spend on publicity will depend on whom you are trying to attract and the location of the venue. If you are in a high street gallery with good passing trade you may not need a great deal of publicity; if you are exhibiting in a lesser known venue you may need to spend a considerable amount to ensure that people visit the exhibition.
- *Mail shots*. If you already have a customer database you will need to make sure that you send an invitation to all these people, in addition to critics, other gallery owners, potential customers and anyone who might stage another exhibition.
- *Hire of equipment*. Not all venues will be able to provide exactly the type of display stands and lighting that you require. It is important that goods are displayed properly so allow for the hire of equipment in your budget.
- *Private view*. Most exhibitions hold a private view prior to the opening of the exhibition. This is when collectors, past customers, friends, relatives, influential people and the press are invited for a glass of wine and some light refreshments. The scale of this will depend on the venue and whom you are trying to attract.

Negotiations

When negotiating an exhibition use the exhibition checklist so that you know exactly where you stand. Most venues that have regular exhibitions will have agreement forms for you to sign. Only you can decide whether the terms are suitable but if the agreement is very complicated and difficult to understand do check with a solicitor before signing.

Checklist for an exhibition agreement

Details of the following should appear in any exhibition agreement. This may seem to be very formal, but will ensure that your rights are protected.

- Names and addresses of all parties.
- Identification of works to be exhibited: descriptions and prices. Also, details of any types of work which must *not* be included, if applicable.
- The location, gallery hours and details of exhibition space.
- The duration of the exhibition.
- Details of the private view or reception: the date, time and where the responsibility for costs lies.
- Publicity: who is responsible for advertising, catalogues, photographs and so on, and who will pay the costs involved?
- What the venue expects the craftworker to provide in the way of promotional literature.
- How much time does the gallery expect the artist to spend at the exhibition?
- Responsibility for packing, freight and insurance from studio to gallery and gallery to studio, and from gallery to customer, if appropriate.
- General insurance cover details (amount, dates valid etc.).

- Preparation and hanging time available.
- Conditions of sale: if all goods will be for sale, who is responsible for setting the prices and collecting the money?
- Details of the payment of artist or craftworker: timing and statements.
- Arrangements for unsold work.
- Whether you are allowed to exhibit in other venues during this period.
- Copyright: will the copyright for any promotional images remain with you after the exhibition or will the venue retain rights over them?
- This agreement should be signed and dated.

Organising an exhibition

Dates

It is important to time the exhibition as carefully as possible. If you are exhibiting in a gallery for the first time, you may find that you have to accept the dates that they offer and then try and arrange a better date for next year.

Planning the workload

You need to ensure that you will have enough work for the exhibition. This can act as a useful discipline for craftworkers who are not very focused, but can be difficult for those who panic when faced with deadlines. You will also need to allow time for organising the exhibition. A commercial gallery may undertake to do this for you, but you will still have to supply them with customer lists and other information.

The private view

This is a time when invited individuals can view the work in private, meet the craftworker or artist and hopefully buy before the general public is allowed to view. You need to send a lot more invitations out than the number of people that you expect to come. You can obviously rely on friends and family to support you, but critics and potential customers might not be so obliging. Invitations are never wasted; even if people don't come to the private view they may well visit the exhibition at another time.

When compiling a guest list ask the venue manager if he keeps a guest list. You should also include: other gallery owners; local art and design college staff; art association officials; advisers such as bank managers; friends and family; your existing customers; local personalities; and members of the press.

Display

Good display is vital, as a poor display will spoil the best objects. You do not need to spend a lot of money on expensive display items – care and attention to detail are more important – but don't compromise on good lighting. Check the display regularly throughout the exhibition. Provide professional labelling either using a computer or ask a friend who does calligraphy to help. These should contain the maker's name, the date it was made, details of the process, the catalogue number (if used), and the selling price. If you are borrowing any items specifically for the exhibition do remember to credit the owner and state clearly that the items are on loan.

Insurance

If the venue does not provide insurance, make sure that you are covered under your own policy or take out additional cover.

Title

Choosing a good title is important. Don't assume that people know your work. 'Ceramics by Chris Smith' immediately tells people what is on display. 'New Work by Chris Smith' does not.

Publicity

Posters, advertisements, press releases and mail shots will be the main sources of publicity. Printed posters are expensive but effective - if you can design your own and use a local print shop this will cut costs. Before deciding on the size of posters, think about where you intend to display them - many places will only accept A4 size, so offering larger posters is a waste of time. You may be able to arrange joint advertising with the venue. They should publicise your exhibition in their literature, otherwise an advertisement in your local paper will probably be sufficient. Press releases are very important. They should be sent to all the local press, local radio, etc. See Chapter 15 for ideas on how to prepare and distribute them. If you keep a customer list then you need to mail shot them - for a large or first exhibition you might consider purchasing a mailing list. Don't forget to put a visitors' book on display and/or a box for business cards, as this will enable you to build a list of interested people for future exhibitions.

The catalogue

A catalogue is basically a list of the products in the exhibition, although it can be much more. It should have details of the craftworker, his background, and any previous exhibitions and commissions. You could consider having a general brochure printed, using a separate printed list of exhibits at each exhibition. Colour postcards are good publicity items which people can take home to remind them of your work since attractive cards like these are often kept and pinned on boards, keeping your work in focus. You should also have photographs available for the press; newspapers will often send a reporter but not a photographer.

Exhibiting at short notice

Sometimes opportunities arise for you to exhibit at short notice. It may seem a wonderful opportunity, but if you don't have your best work available, or have to rush your work, be very wary. A badly-prepared exhibition can be very damaging, as having insufficient work on display or time to publicise may damage your reputation.

After the exhibition

Always thank everyone who has helped, and keep records of attendances, catalogue sales and so on for future reference. If you have received financial assistance, the people who helped you may need to see copies of your accounts.

The gallery owner will probably expect you to return the space to the condition in which you found it. This may mean filling holes and rubbing down, even painting if necessary. Taking down an exhibition is not much fun but it needs to be done properly if you are to expect a second invitation. Remember that the event organisers may want to start the next exhibition almost immediately so you will have to remove things fairly quickly.

Straight after an exhibition it is a good idea to make some notes about what happened, what sold, and how you could do things differently next time. You may well forget all this by the time the next exhibition comes around.

Don't forget to deliver the work to your buyers, if this is part of the deal. Ring them first and arrange a time – don't risk leaving a parcel on the porch when they could be away on holiday!

The result

Hopefully you will have sold some of your work, gained some commissions and made some good contacts. You may also have been approached by another venue for a future exhibition and you will have an enhanced reputation.

Chapter 13:

Networking

Communication has never been easier: with the Internet and mobile phones you never need to feel 'alone'. Yet many artists do work in isolation, and the marketing of their work suffers as a consequence. Keeping in touch with other artists, craftworkers and organisations which are likely to be of assistance in growing your business is vital. You will benefit from the exchange of ideas and support that is available, and will find reassurance in talking to other people in your situation.

Unless you plug into the networks in your area you will miss out on opportunities to market your work, enter for exhibitions, and find out what is going on in your field.

What is a network?

A network is simply a group of people who communicate with each other, support each other and help each other with their work. If you share studio space, or work in a craft centre, then you will find it easier to keep in contact and there will be a natural exchange of information. If you work alone then you will have to make some effort to maintain these contacts. Ways of doing this include joining a craft guild or association, subscribing to a publication or even using the Internet.

Your immediate network

When you start out in crafts, don't forget to make use of your immediate network: family, friends, colleagues and neighbours can all be used to spread the word that you are now in business and making a product. Let all these people know when you are visiting your first craft fair. Hopefully they will all come along and may even buy something. Remember you will need all the friends you can get to help you become established.

Expanding your contacts

To ensure that you receive current information, the first thing to do is to make sure that your name is on all the appropriate mailing lists. All arts boards and associations, and the Crafts Council, keep lists of craftworkers to whom they regularly send information. If you attend craft fairs you need to be on the organisers' lists.

Craft guilds and associations

There may be a craft guild in your area – ask at your local arts council or library. If it holds events regularly then the Tourist Information Service may have its address. The Crafts Council keeps a list of guilds, and craft publications often feature or list guilds. To find out about the effectiveness of guilds you need to ask the members. Some exist mainly to promote the craft educationally, others to provide a market for their members' crafts.

Some guilds accept work from all types of craftworker and it is simply a matter of turning up and asking to join. Others are very strict about membership and will want to see samples of your work. Some guilds only accept one type of craft. Just occasionally a guild will only admit one member for each craft. This can be disappointing, but if it organises fairs it may want to present a wide range of different crafts.

There are over 200 guilds in the UK, so there will probably be one near you that is suitable. Before joining, decide what you want from a guild. Do you want an outlet for your product, or do you want the status that a specific guild might give you? Check out the benefits of membership, any training offered, how often members meet, and their fees.

You may benefit from belonging to a local guild with different crafts *and* a national guild for your specific craft. This should give you access to the widest range of services.

Guilds do rely on their members to perform a lot of the functions, so if you want your guild to be a success then be prepared to play your part in helping the organisation.

Arts organisations

There are arts organisations covering all types of media. Local art societies tend to concentrate on the more traditional work. In regional societies, standards tend to be higher and sometimes you have to be invited to join. Some artists' organisations offer reduced insurance and they may be worth joining to be able to benefit from this and other help.

The more prestigious arts organisations are only open by invitation. You may be offered an invitation when you become established and develop a good reputation. The best way of coming to the attention of this type of organisation is by entering the exhibitions they stage.

Small business organisations

For craftworkers who wish to build a more commercial type of business it may be useful to belong to a small business organisation. Organisations such as the Forum for Private Business and the Federation of Small Businesses provide their members with discounted insurance and free legal help lines which can add up to considerable savings. Locally, there may be a small business club which you might find useful. There are also special organisations for women in business and sometimes young people in business.

Take advantage of invitations to meetings by taking your business cards and talking to as many people as possible. Some people do not always find this easy, but it does get easier with practice and can prove very rewarding for the business.

Copyright

If you believe that your goods are likely to be copied then it is a good idea to join one of the organisations which help protect against this unfortunate practice. The main organisations are ACID (Anti-Copyright In Design) and Copywatch, which is administered by The Giftware Association.

Publications

Subscribing to a regular publication can be a vital lifeline, providing up-to-date information on your craft, the general market and opportunities. There are many publications which may be appropriate for you. If you don't know where to start, check out the following:

- *The Craftsman Magazine*
- *Crafts*
- *The Craftworker's Yearbook*
- *The Artist's Newsletter*
- *Ceramic Review*
- *The Artist*
- *Artist and Illustrator*

Your professional support network

At different stages of building a business you will need help from professionals: solicitors, accountants and arts administrators may all be of use to you and it is important to cultivate a good relationship with them.

Finding people you can trust and who talk your language is vital. Ask friends or other craftworkers to recommend an accountant or a solicitor if you need one. If you don't know anyone, ring up a firm and explain the type of business you are running and ask to meet someone. The initial consultation should be free and one of the most important things to ascertain is whether you feel comfortable with the adviser and able to trust him.

If you belong to a craft scheme or the Prince's Trust you may be given the services of a mentor. Again, it is important that you feel comfortable with this person and able to talk to him if you are going to get the most benefit from the relationship. Don't be afraid to ask for someone else if the relationship isn't working.

Chapter 14:

Advertising

Many craftworkers do not feel comfortable with advertising, perhaps due to unhappy past experiences or the fact that it is difficult to monitor the results and ascertain the level of 'value for money'. Lord Leverhulme is quoted as having said, "Half the money I spend on advertising is wasted. My problem is to find out which half".

Advertising *does* work. It has been proved that sales tend to fall away when the advertising stops. The link is there, but actually providing accurate measurements for a particular advertisement is difficult.

The advantage of advertising over other forms of promotion, such as Public Relations, is that you have direct control over exactly what is published and when it is published. This can be very important, particularly if you are launching a new product or opening a studio and want to link various types of promotion. Reckless spending on advertising is foolish. What is needed is a properly thought-out campaign with definite objectives.

Successful advertising

To be successful an advertising campaign requires a series of carefully planned advertisements, which are part of an overall promotional scheme. To succeed with advertising you need to know the four Ws: WHY, WHO, WHERE and WHEN.

- *Why* you are advertising.
- *Who* you are targeting.
- *Where* you intend to advertise.
- *When* you want to advertise.

Reasons for advertising

- To attract new buyers.
- To announce a new product.
- To highlight a promotion.
- To attract stockists.
- To educate and/or inform.
- To increase/build customer loyalty.
- To create confidence in a product.
- To back up your sales force.

How much to spend

Deciding the size of the advertising budget is very difficult. A new studio may need to spend heavily to establish a presence in the market. A more established one may only need to reinforce its position. Experience is the best guide. Inevitably, you will be influenced by how much you can afford, but you need to remember that you cannot afford *not* to advertise. The advertising budget will be part of the promotional budget, which will also include exhibitions and special events. Decide how much you intend to spend over the next year and stick to your budget. Do not be tempted to cut back if sales improve, although if one advert is performing better than the others it may be worth re-allocating resources.

How to write an advertisement

When you write an advertisement always try and focus on your customers. What do they need to know? Remember you will only have a few seconds to make an impact on them. Good advertisements follow the AIDA formula:

- *Attention* - can be aroused by a headline and/or picture.
- *Interest* - the copy must be of interest.
- *Desire* - persuade the customer that he really wants your product.
- *Action* - include something extra to spur the customer on to buying, for example a money-off coupon or trial offer.

Use a professional approach and draw up a 'creative brief'. The main points to be covered are:

- The *objectives* - what do you want to achieve?
- The *target audience* - who are the customers?
- The *Unique Selling Proposition* - what is the main benefit of the product?
- The *supporting evidence* - the facts and figures.

To create advertising copy, write down the answers to the following questions:

- How is it made?
- What does it do?

- What does it look like? (A picture may be essential.)
- Does it save money?
- Is it valuable?
- Is it fashionable?
- Does it offer good value for money?
- Is it collectable?

Use the words you have written down to create an advertisement, taking into account the type of customer you wish to attract. For example, 'funky jewellery' is suitable for young people, whereas 'a gift to cherish' will appeal to a more mature customer. Look at your competitors' advertising. What works and what doesn't? Use this as a guide. However, remember you must not steal advertising copy (e.g. slogans, pictures, phrases or arrangement). This is copyright protected, but there is no copyright in ideas.

Publishers of advertising media will always offer to help you with the layout of your advertisement and the introduction of pictures, if you lack the skills and/or equipment to do this yourself. If you choose to let them lay out your ad, you must insist on a proof in good time so you can be sure how it will look.

Where to advertise

- Local paper – if you want to attract people to your studio.
- Craft fair brochures – to ensure customers visit your stand.
- Craft magazines – for new stockists.
- Interiors magazines – for direct sales.
- County magazines – for upmarket customers.

The Internet

Advertising on the Internet is becoming increasingly popular amongst craftworkers, but as yet no research has been carried out as to its effectiveness. Crafts are a very tactile product and most customers like to handle the work, at least initially. However, as you become more established, a website should help to increase sales, raise your profile and encourage people to visit your studio.

There are many designated craft sites on the Internet which you can join. A brief search will show you the possibilities. Costs for setting up a website vary and, as with all purchases, always shop around and obtain several quotes.

One way in which the Internet is proving very useful is in providing information for craftworkers. A regular visit to the Arts Council site can provide information on current developments and highlight opportunities for commissions. See the Resource File on page 186 for some helpful websites.

Chapter 15:

Public Relations

What is PR?

Few people understand the nature and value of Public Relations. It is often seen as free advertising when, in fact, it is about helping you to create a positive image in the press and to keep your customers informed about what is happening to you. If you win an award, are exhibiting at an unusual venue, or produce a new product, then PR can help you to tell your customers about it.

It can help your business if you acquire and retain a good reputation. It can also improve the image of the business and it can be useful in countering any negative publicity. Small businesses often dismiss Public Relations as being irrelevant to their needs, but all businesses have a 'public'. Your public could include your suppliers, creditors, authorities, customers and potential customers and, as it is an extremely cost-effective method of influencing people, it should be used as widely as possible. A glance at your local newspaper or trade press will show which craftworkers are adept at using PR. Are you losing out to your rivals?

There is no magic to PR; any craftworker can practise it. You can teach yourself how to use PR to your advantage; in fact, you may already be using some of the techniques without being aware of the fact. PR is simply about building a relationship with the press, learning to write a press release and promoting your business in the media at every opportunity.

Measuring the benefits of PR is very difficult, but after a well-planned PR campaign it should be possible to see the benefits in increased market share, customer loyalty, staff morale, recruitment and a general increased awareness of your products.

An added advantage of PR is that people tend to believe what they read in an article or news item more than they do an advertisement. Readers have 'trust' in journalists. You will also reach people you wouldn't normally target and this can be very positive for a growing business. Living and working in a media-dominated society, it is foolish not to use all possible methods to communicate your business's message.

The press release

One of the easiest and most effective methods of contacting the media is with a press release. This is a written statement from a person or organisation containing news of and all the details about a forthcoming event or promotion. A press release should be attractive and readily usable by reporters. It should, as far as possible, be written in the style of the publication. For example, a press release for a trade journal may contain technical data, which would be of little interest to a local paper.

The main ingredients of a press release are:

Headline This should give some indication as to the content of the press release. There is no need to try and think of some clever phrase, as most reporters prefer to write their own headlines when filing a story.

Beginning As with a good book, the first line is very important and needs to catch the reader's attention straight away.

The facts A press release should contain the 'five Ws': *Who, What, Where, When* and *Why*.

Quotes Always try and give the story a personal angle. A quote from a satisfied customer is useful, as is a photograph of the people involved.

Example of a press release

John Jones Jeweller

PRESS RELEASE

(Date)
For immediate release

LOCAL TV STAR TO OPEN JEWELLERY EXHIBITION

An exhibition of jewellery by **John Jones** will be opened by local television personality **Chris Smith** on Friday 1st June at 10 am. Chris Smith is well known for his appearances as art critic on our regional news programme.

The exhibition features jewellery commissioned by Anytown Art Gallery for sale in their new shop. The designs of the jewellery are based on local architecture and feature well-known landmarks. The silver jewellery has also won the

Watson Award from the Regional Arts Board for innovation. Local MP and Arts Minister, **Laura Lewis**, will present the award at the launch.

Sir Andy Walker, Chairman of the Gallery, said, "We are delighted with this range of jewellery – it is the first time we have commissioned work of this nature and we believe that it will be a great success".

John Jones has a studio at Anytown Craft Centre. He trained at Anytown University, where he gained an MA in Fine Art and Design. He has worked on commissions for other art galleries, but this is the first time he has won an award.

The exhibition will be held in the main hall of the Art Gallery at Portland Street, Anytown, and after the launch will be open from 9 am to 6 pm every day until Sunday 10th June.

For further information and interviews, contact:
Sally White, PR Officer, Anytown Art Gallery,
Tel: 01111 111111

John Jones, Anytown Craft Centre, Tel: 01111 222222

Advantages of using a press release

There are many advantages in using a written press release. The main ones are:

- As it is in writing, you have a permanent record of its contents.
- An over-zealous reporter does not pressure you in person or on the phone.
- You can control the timing of the press release. Not all journalists honour embargo dates so, if it is very

sensitive, send it out after the event.

- It is very cost-effective.
- It is helpful to journalists as it provides the facts in a simple and clear format.

Having established the advantages of a press release, you must remember that editors receive thousands of press releases every month, so to get yours used it should have two extra things:

1. It should be written in journalistic style.
2. It should be newsworthy – find an interesting angle and you should be guaranteed success.

In order to persuade a journalist to print your story you will need an 'angle', something that makes your product or company newsworthy. No matter how good your relationship is with the journalist, he is not going to risk his reputation by publishing dull and uninteresting news.

Rules for writing a press release

1. Use eye-catching paper, something that attracts attention without detracting from the message.
2. Use simple words and short sentences.
3. Avoid jargon and acronyms – unless writing for the trade press.
4. If you must use them, make sure all trade and technical terms are correct.
5. Keep it as short as possible. One side of A4, with an extra page of background if necessary, is ideal.
6. Write only on one side of the paper.

7. Use wide margins, double spacing and a clear typeface.
8. Finish the release with a contact name and number.
9. Choose a positive headline.
10. Answer the five Ws, preferably in the first paragraph.
11. Write news not views.
12. Always double-check spelling of names.
13. If the press release is not for immediate publication, state the embargo date.
14. Include a good quotation, if possible.
15. Include a good black and white photograph, if possible. Clearly label it and identify all the subjects in the photograph.
16. Send it to the right person. A telephone call to the publication's office will tell you who deals with your subject.
17. Keep a copy of everything you send, and a note of to whom it was sent.

Where to send your press release

To maximise the effect of your promotion you need to send press releases to the most appropriate media. In choosing the right media you need to consider their needs and customers, as well as your own. There is a vast range of publications available, covering every conceivable subject. Newsagents, even the major ones, carry only a fraction of the journals available. To find out the names of publications and their addresses you need to consult a copy of *BRAD*. This is a monthly publication which lists every newspaper, business journal, consumer publication, independent TV and commercial radio station in the UK. Most large public libraries keep a copy.

If you feel that you have a story of major importance you can send a press release to: The Press Association, 292 Vauxhall Bridge Road, London, SW1V 1AE. They provide a news service for virtually all newspapers, radio and television. Otherwise, consider the following:

LOCAL NEWSPAPERS

This is probably the best place to start, as they are always looking for local news with human interest. The installation of a new machine will not usually merit much attention, but if its production creates jobs, or if a member of staff has to fly to America for training, they may well be interested. Usually, local newspapers work a week or two in advance.

TRADE PRESS

There is a wide variety of newspapers and magazines which rarely appear on newsagent shelves. These are often distributed free or under subscription to members of a particular trade. These publications rely on press releases to keep them up-to-date with developments. Read them carefully and decide which section your press release will fit into: 'new products', appointments, exhibitions or features. Their deadline for copy will probably be earlier than the local press, so make sure that you send the information in time for publication.

CONSUMER MAGAZINES

These magazines do not generally contain many news items. Their deadline date for editorial is usually two or three months before production. Contacting the advertising department for a list of future features could lead you to find a connection with your product. Some of these magazines will give you editorial space if you advertise, so it is always worth trying to negotiate this if their readers are particularly important to you.

NATIONAL AND REGIONAL NEWSPAPERS

To stand any possibility of being mentioned in national or regional newspapers your story will need to have a wider appeal. Any connection with a current news story obviously helps. With such a wide circulation any mention of your promotion will be valuable. Many local reporters feed stories to the regional and national newspapers, so you may find your story appearing in other publications via this method. These larger papers may work between a couple of days to a week in advance.

LOCAL RADIO

This attracts the same sort of audience as local newspapers and can be a very effective medium. However, before approaching the radio station you need to have someone prepared and able to be interviewed. If the station is running a promotion you might be able to link in. They also often cover local events, so if you are sponsoring one don't forget to invite them. They may even broadcast from there if the event is interesting enough and if they are given a few weeks' notice.

TELEVISION

To attract television attention your story will need to have a strong visual content. Regional news programmes will often cover stories concerning celebrities or dramatic events, if given sufficient notice. You should never rely on television coverage – if a major news story breaks on the day you were due to appear, you may end up on the cutting room floor. If you really want television coverage, try and schedule your promotion for quiet times, such as the first week in January or during the summer holiday break. Do not dismiss television as being too grand – it is a very persuasive medium and even the smallest mention can be very effective.

Contacting the press

Contact with the press is a two-way process. It is no use expecting them to help you and publicise your events if you run for cover at the first sign of trouble. Journalists soon tire of people who expect them to help one minute, and then respond with 'no comment' when asked about staff cuts.

When talking to a journalist, always assume that anything you say will appear in print. You need to know the journalist very well before you can talk 'off the record'. Sensitive issues are best handled by prepared statements and it can be a good idea to practise writing these before a crisis actually occurs.

Building up a good relationship with the press during the good times can prove invaluable when things go wrong. The company that produces Perrier water realised the value of a good public image when it had to withdraw a batch of contaminated bottled water. If the company had not had such a positive image it would not have been able to recover its market position so quickly and successfully.

Worrying about being misreported and losing control of a campaign is natural, but your confidence to work with the press will grow as you become more experienced. Initially, you will probably be dealing with local newspapers and radio, as well as the trade press, rather than the national dailies that are looking for the more 'exciting' type of story. Some publications have a reputation of misquoting people and treating them badly. Try and avoid contact with them, particularly if your business is suffering from the type of problems which appeal to this type of publication. The best action is to say nothing and, if the situation demands it, contact a solicitor to speak on your behalf.

Some publications will only accept editorial from advertisers – this can work to your advantage and disadvantage. If you would advertise in the publication anyway then it is probably worth negotiating a deal, otherwise decline politely.

Always remember:

- DON'T attempt to mislead the media with false claims.
- DON'T expect preferential treatment if you advertise. They have a product to sell as well and will use the best material available.
- DON'T expect editors to be as excited as you are about your promotion.
- DON'T leave everything to the last minute and then expect immediate action.
- DON'T over-promote the name of the company or product.
- DON'T forget to thank them if they use your release.
- DON'T try and bribe the journalist.

What to promote

You may have decided that PR seems like a good idea but cannot think of anything about your business that could be promoted. Consider what makes a good story:

- Relevance to the medium's readership/customers.
- Human interest.
- Topicality.
- Timing.
- Entertainment value, originality or humour.
- Availability of good photos.

So, what can you offer? Have you recently changed your product? Is it a new development? Have you changed name so you can sell it abroad? Won an award? Has one of your staff recently done something interesting? Are you employing more staff? In times of recession, good news is particularly welcome. Are you taking part in a special event or promotion?

Chapter 16:

Using Technology

Those people who predicted that the rise of the computer would be the end of creative industries couldn't have been more wrong. Creative people are using computer technology to cut costs, improve efficiency and increase profits. Success isn't entirely dependent on having access to a computer, but it can help.

Keeping in touch

In other parts of this book I have stressed the importance of keeping in touch and finding out what is going on in your field. Visit the websites of the Arts Council, the Crafts Council and *The Artist's Newsletter* regularly and you can pick up a lot of information. During the Foot and Mouth crisis, when craft fairs were being cancelled, many craftworkers found that by getting their information over the Internet they were able to reorganise their year and take advantage of alternative venues very quickly. See the Resource File, page 186, for some useful websites.

Selling your work on the web

There is still some debate as to whether art and craft sells well via the Internet. Used in conjunction with other selling methods, there is no doubt that the web can increase sales and put you in touch with more customers. It can enhance your reputation and allow people to see a larger selection of your work than would otherwise be possible. It can also enable your work to reach people who would not hear about you any other way. For instance, a landscape artist in Lancashire received a commission from an American collector who visited her website and wanted a painting of a particular local scene. It is hard to know how she could have achieved this sale by any other means.

To exhibit your work over the Internet you will need a website. You can set up your own, or exhibit on someone else's. This book is not the place to teach you how to design a website – if it is a particular interest of yours then you can go on a course to learn how to do it. Otherwise, find a friend who knows what he is doing or employ professionals. Trying to do it yourself can take up time which would be better spent on other aspects of your business. A word of warning – there are a lot of cowboys in this business, so try and use someone who has been personally recommended, or ask at your local Enterprise Agency. Sometimes packages are available at very competitive prices.

Directing people to your website

Once you have your website set up, it needs to be easily accessed via search engines. This service will probably be available from your website designer, or you can contact the search engines yourself and ask to be added to their database. If your intention is to sell from the site then your site simply must be visible. You will need to find ways of directing people onto the site in addition to the search engines. It is a good idea to put the address of your website on all your promotional material.

In order to be accepted by a search engine the content of your site must be clear and well-written. The popularity of the site is also vital, and the more links you have to other sites the better. If you belong to a group of artists then setting up a site together or having links to each other's sites could be mutually beneficial.

Making sales

Setting up a system to allow people to purchase goods via your website can be very expensive and, unless this is expected to be your main method of marketing, is probably not a good idea. You could include an order form on your website which can be printed off and then sent through the post with a cheque. If you can take credit card orders over the telephone then people can be encouraged to order in this way. However, research has shown that if people cannot purchase immediately then they often lose interest, so you will have to work out whether the setting-up costs are worthwhile. If your work is available over the Internet from other sources, like galleries, then it is probably best to let them do the selling while you concentrate on promoting your work.

Using a scanner

Using a computer to produce letterheads and brochures, for example, is a very cost-effective way of doing things. With the addition of a scanner you can widen the scope of your activities. Scanned-in photographs can be used in promoting your work and it is also possible, using even the most basic scanner, to scan in products such as jewellery or textiles. Pieces of jewellery, placed flat and then covered with fabric, can produce really effective images. If you have a scanner, play around with it and try manipulating the images using a program like Adobe Photoshop.

Depending on your type of work, you may need to have the images professionally scanned onto a CD. This service is now available from an increasing number of printers, some of whom will also photograph the work first if necessary. Once you have a digital image of your work you can use it on posters to advertise exhibitions, on cards to sell, or for prints which can be framed and sold.

CD ROM

An increasing number of galleries are asking to see work on CD ROMs. For this you will need to purchase, or have access to, a CD Writer. The CDs can be given out at trade shows or sent to galleries. It is a good way of letting people see a lot of your work very quickly. However, don't assume that a gallery will automatically use this method to view work - always include traditional material as well.

Producing prints on your computer

A process that has revolutionised the way we make prints is Giclee - French for 'to spray ink'. It creates an inkjet print, produced on a high quality, large format inkjet printer. The results are close to the original and have opened up the print market to a wider number of artists. This still needs to be carried out by a professional printer, but it does mean that short print runs are economical.

You can also produce your own prints at home. The Epson 2000P printer, for example, utilises 'archival' pigmented inks which Epson claims are lightfast for 100 years. These inks are intended for use in conjunction with artist grade inkjet papers, which are now widely available.

If you are interested in investing in the equipment and enjoy this side of the business you can sometimes do work for other artists as an extra source of income.

This technology is improving all the time and a visit to your local computer store should tell you what is available.

Case Studies

---

1. 'Island Heritage' – producers of hand-knitted goods

Penny Webb runs a craft business, producing hand-knitted goods in wool from rare breeds of sheep. She buys fleeces from Scotland and the Isle of Man and then makes them into garments to sell, often back to the place of origin. Penny mainly supplies small knitwear shops.

Penny's business could be located virtually anywhere, as she mainly sells to retailers and export buyers. She was fortunate enough to be able to convert premises on her family farm for her work, and she also sells directly from a shop on the farm.

She exports 40 per cent of her wholesale production and receives most of her export orders by exhibiting at the *Glasgow Trade Fair*. She has not yet exhibited abroad, but intends to do so in the near future. Abroad, her main customers are shops specialising in Scottish goods. She exports to America, Japan, Germany, Holland and Austria. The only problems she has encountered are with some of her American buyers who have not acknowledged the pro-forma invoices she has sent following the placing of an order. Her buyers in Germany and Holland are more difficult - they want individually hand-crafted goods, yet complain if they are not all identical!

2. 'Ceramic Swine' - makers of ceramics

Christine Cummings is a very successful studio potter. She was the first winner of the *Craftsman Newcomers Gallery Award* at the *British Craft Trade Fair* and since then she has enjoyed a full order book. However, when she started working in pottery she had to work in the mornings on her parents' farm, picking lettuces to make some money to support her craft.

She specialises in ceramic pigs, based on rare breeds. She has definitely discovered a 'niche' market. To ensure that her designs are accurate, she seeks help from pig breeders. Christine says, "I find it much more satisfying to capture the 'warts and all-ness' of a floppy sow, rather than the cuteness of a piglet. I work in stoneware clay, raku and smoke-fire the final pieces". She has work on sale in some of the major galleries in the UK and is now looking to the export market.

3. 'Wired' - makers of steel candlesticks and furniture

Twelve years' experience in sheet metal fabrication and welding in a factory hardly seems like an appropriate training ground for someone now running a successful business. But David Channell has changed worlds and now trades with his brother Leighton as 'Wired', exhibiting their work at a large number of fairs all over the UK. The first pieces they made were a selection of candleholders, which were given away as Christmas presents - a familiar story for many fledgling craftworkers.

Most of his competitors' products are imported – so it is amazing that David has taken on the import market and won, in a real David and Goliath situation! He puts his success down to the better quality and higher level of design of his products, which are nonetheless priced competitively.

'Wired' was originally based at the Belgrave Business Enterprise Centre in Leicester (an old factory building which was redeveloped into twenty-four small units for business start-ups), but has now moved to larger premises. David successfully applied for a loan through a local trust called the Thomas White Foundation. He put together a business plan and a formal proposal to develop his business and was delighted when everything was approved and the grant offered. He used the funding to invest in machinery and promotional material.

4. Liam Spencer – artist

Liam started working as an artist with the help of the Enterprise Allowance Scheme in 1989. Although he has previously had to supplement his income with part-time work, he is now able to support himself solely on the sales of his paintings.

In addition to his own work, he administers a group studio in Manchester. He believes that it is very useful to belong to an artists' group as you can support each other, and the contacts you make can really open doors for you.

Working in the city centre is important to Liam as his work is based on the urban landscapes he sees from his studio. He recently had the opening exhibition at *The Lowry* in Salford, which was completely sold out. He achieved this exhibition by a speculative approach to the gallery when it was being built. Several galleries take his work on a regular basis and he has had several solo exhibitions.

He says, "I am very aware of the value of publicity but, as with most artists, I find it difficult to 'sell myself'. I believe that the value of good publicity material should not be underestimated. Good photographs, well-designed business cards and a brochure do not always cost a lot, but if they reflect the quality of your work they will impress galleries".

5. Ian M Emberson – artist and writer

Ian spent his working life as a music librarian in Huddersfield. During this time he wrote poetry, having five volumes published. Early retirement has allowed him to devote more time to his painting and writing. As an artist, he has had many solo exhibitions and has also illustrated his own poetry and other collections. His work is in the fantasy genre and his drawings are often based on drawings which he has kept from his childhood.

He originally produced postcards to go with an exhibition and found they sold well. He now has a range which he distributes through 16 different outlets, ranging from a textile mill to bars and gift shops. He believes that post cards are a wonderful way of getting your work known, but cautions that your best paintings are not necessarily the ones which sell well as postcards. Sometimes just a section of the work will make a good image. He takes his own photographs of his work using natural light and a long exposure, and has always found this to be successful.

Resource File

General

Anti-Copying in Design (ACID)
150 Aldersgate Street
London
EC1 4EJ
Tel: 020 7794 2173

Copywatch – the Giftware Association
10 Vyse Street
Birmingham
B18 6LT
Tel: 0121 236 2657

The Crafts Council
44a Pentonville Road
Islington
London
N1 9BY
General enquiries tel: 020 7806 2501
Bookshop tel: 020 7806 2559

This is the national body for promoting contemporary crafts. It provides information on all aspects of crafts throughout the UK. It runs the national centre for crafts which houses the Gallery, Gallery Shop, Reference Library and Picture Library.

The Office of the Data Protection Registrar
Wycliffe House
Water Lane
Wilmslow
Cheshire
SK9 5AF
Tel: 01625 545745

Arts organisations

All arts organisations have a Visual Arts Officer who is responsible for crafts.

East England Arts
Eden House
48-49 Baleman Street
Cambridge
CB2 1LR
Tel: 01223 454400

East Midlands Arts
Mountfields House
Epinal Way
Loughborough
Leicestershire
LE11 0QE
Tel: 01509 218292

Crafts Council of Ireland
Castle Yard
Kilkenny
Eire
Tel: 00 353 56 61804

London Arts
2 Peartree Court
London
EC1R 0DS
Tel: 020 7608 6100

North West Arts Board
Manchester House
22 Bridge Street
Manchester
M3 3AB
Tel: 0161 834 6644

Northern Arts
Central Square
Forth Street
Newcastle Upon Tyne
Tyne & Wear
NE1 3PJ
Tel: 0191 255 8500

South East Arts
10 Mount Ephraim
Tunbridge Wells
Kent
TN4 8AS
Tel: 01892 515210

South West Arts
Bradnich Place
Gandy Street
Exeter
Devon
EX4 3LS
Tel: 01392 218188

Southern Arts
13 St Clement Street
Winchester
Hampshire
SO23 9DQ
Tel: 01962 855099

West Midlands Arts
82 Granville Street
Birmingham
West Midlands
B1 2LH
Tel: 0121 631 3121

Yorkshire Arts
21 Bond Street
Dewsbury
West Yorkshire
WF13 1AX
Tel: 01924 455555

Small Business Organisations

Every region has its own Business Link, which is part of the Small Business Service. Your local telephone directory will have a contact number, or you can visit their website at www.sbs.gov.uk

Federation of Small Businesses
Whittle Way
Blackpool Business Park
Blackpool
FY4 2FE
Tel: 01253 336000

The Forum of Private Business
Ruskin Chambers
Drury Lane
Knutsford
Cheshire
WA16 6HA
Tel: 01565 634467

ICOM (Industrial Common Ownership Movement)
74 Kirkgate
Leeds
LS2 7DJ
Tel: 0113 246 1737

This is the national federation for worker co-operatives, development agencies and supporters.

The Small Business Bureau
46 Westminster Palace Gardens
Artillery Row
London
SW1P 1RR
Tel: 020 7976 7262

Special Groups

Shell Livewire
Hawthorn House
Forth Banks
Newcastle Upon Tyne
NE1 3SG
Tel: 0845 757 3252

Offers free information for people aged 16 to 30 who are starting their own business and organises an award scheme.

The Prince's Trust
18 Park Square East
London
NW1 4LH
Tel: 0800 842842

Craft Fairs

For a full list of current fairs see The Craftsman Magazine *(page 185).*

Art in Action
96 Sedlescombe Road
London
SW6 1RB
Tel: 020 7381 3192

Holds annual exhibitions for artists and craftworkers. There is a great emphasis on demonstrations at their events.

Channel Islands National Craft Fairs
National House
28 Grosvenor Road
Richmond
Surrey
TW10 6PD
Tel: 020 8940 4608

Organiser of fairs in the Channel Islands and the UK.

Cheshire Fayre
PO Box 51
Macclesfield
Cheshire
SK10 4EL
Tel: 01625 430519

Organises fairs in the north-west of England.

Countrywide Events
10 Naseby Drive
Loughborough
Leicestershire
LE11 4NU
Tel: 01509 217444

Well promoted events which attract good visitor numbers.

County Crafts
PO Box 2
Ratby
Leicestershire
LE6 0XT
Tel: 01162 394366

Organises fairs at indoor venues and outdoor family events, mainly in the Midlands.

The Craft Movement
PO Box 1641
Frome
Somerset
BA11 1YY
Tel: 01373 813333

Organises fairs all over the country for craftworkers of any discipline.

The Exhibition Team Ltd
Events House
Wycombe Air Park
Booker
Marlow
Buckinghamshire
SL7 3DP
Tel: 01494 450504

Organisers of general craft fairs and specialist fairs, such as Art in Clay.

Heart of England Craftworkers' Guild
105 St Georges Lane
Worcester
WR1 1QS
Tel: 01905 21702

Have marquees and pavilions at agricultural, equestrian and other outdoor shows and events.

Living Heritage Craft Shows
PO Box 36
Uttoxeter
Staffordshire
ST14 8PY
Tel: 01283 820548

Specialise in craft shows in prestigious venues such as stately homes.

MGA Fairs
PO Box 282
Overstone
Northamptonshire
NN6 0SD
Tel: 0161 860 0755

Organisers of general and specialist teddy bear fairs. They encourage new craftworkers.

Marathon Event Management
The All England Jumping Course
London Road
Hickstead
West Sussex
RH17 5NX
Tel: 01273 833884

Organise the British Craft Trade Fair at Harrogate.

Mary Holland Craft Fairs Ltd
PO Box 43
Abingdon
Oxfordshire
OX14 2EX
Tel: 01235 521873

These shows feature entertainment, competitions and demonstrations.

Oakleigh Craft Fairs
Old Tithe Hall
Start Hill
Bishop's Stortford
Hertfordshire
CM22 7TF
Tel: 01279 871110

Hold two or three day events featuring rural craft demonstrations, children's attractions and entertainment.

Rainbow Fairs
Navigation Wharf
Carre Street
Sleaford
Lincolnshire
NG34 7TW
Tel: 01529 414793

This is one of the longest established fair organisers. They have fairs at major events and stately homes throughout the UK.

Romor Exhibitions
PO Box 448
Bedford
Bedfordshire
MK40 2ZP
Tel: 01234 345725

Organisers of fairs for over 20 years, mainly in the South. Several stately home venues.

Rural Crafts Association
Heights Cottage
Brook Road
Wormley
Godalming
Surrey
GU8 5UA
Tel: 01428 682292

One of the larger, well established organisers. Includes some European venues.

Town and Country Craft Fairs
Hill Cross
Ashford
Bakewell
Derbyshire
DE45 1QL
Tel: 01629 812008

Established organisers in the North and Midlands areas. They also organise specialist teddy bear fairs.

Traditional Crafts Ltd
The Thames Sovereign
Box 31
MBM
Manor Lane
Rochester
Kent
ME1 3HS
Tel: 01634 849778

Organised by craftworkers for craftworkers. All work vetted.

Guilds and Associations

These addresses are correct at the time of publication.

Artists
Association of Illustrators
1st Floor
32-38 Saffron Hill
London
EC1N 8FH
Tel: 020 7613 4328

General
ArtSway
Station Road
Sway
Lymington
Hampshire
SO41 6BA
Tel: 01590 682260

The Art Workers' Guild
6 Queen Square
London
WC1N 3AR

Cornwall Crafts Association
Trelowarren Gallery
Trelowarren
Mawgen-in-Meneage
Helston
Cornwall
TR12 6AF
Tel: 01326 221567

Society of Designer Craftsmen
24 Rivington Street
London
EC2A 3DU
Tel: 01590 670625

Devon Guild of Craftsmen
Riverside Mill
Bovey Tracey
Devon
TQ13 9AF
Tel: 01626 832223

Dorset Craft Guide
17 London Road
Dorchester
Dorset
DT1 1NF

Dyfed Craft Community Co-operative
1 St Mary Street
Guildhall Square
Carmarthen
SA31 1TN

East Sussex Guild of Craftworkers
Little Clays
Willingford Lane
Burwash Weald
Etchingham
East Sussex
TN19 7HR
Tel: 01435 882707

Essex Craft Society
5 Knowles Close
Walstead
Essex
CO9 1BZ
Tel: 01787 473052

Gloucestershire Guild of Craftsmen
The Painswick Centre
Biswick Street
Painswick
GL6 6QQ
Tel: 01452 814745

Guild of Herefordshire Craftsmen
Castle Weir
Lyonshall
Kington
Herefordshire
HR5 4HR

Lincoln and Humberside Contemporary Crafts
The Pearoom
Station Yard
Heckington
Lincolnshire
NG34 9JJ
Tel: 01529 60765

Norfolk Contemporary Craft Society
The White House
Tain Street
Hickling
Norfolk
NR12 0AY
Tel: 01692 598747

Northamptonshire Guild of Designer Craftsmen
28 High Street
Milton Malsor
Northamptonshire
NN7 2AS
Tel: 01604 858470

Nottinghamshire County Crafts
11 Eton Grove
Wollaton Park
Nottinghamshire
NG8 1FT
Tel: 0115 9283 4341

Orchil Craft Association
28 Grant Street
Alloa
Clackmannanshire
FK10 1ND
Tel: 01259 213403

Orkney Craft Industries Association
Outerdykes
Stenness
Orkney
KW16 3HA
Tel: 01856 850207

Oxfordshire Craft Guild
3 Cottesmore Farmhouse
Ewelme
Oxfordshire
OX10 6HQ
Tel: 01491 838048

South Wales Potters
Black Mountain Pottery
Llanlieu Court
Talgarth
LO3 0EB
Tel: 01874 711518

Suffolk Craft Society
Bridge Green Farm
Gissing Road
Burston
Diss
Norfolk
IP22 3UD
Tel: 01379 740711

Surrey Guild of Craftsmen
16 Buckhurst Road
Frimley Green
Camberley
Surrey
GU16 6LH
Tel: 01483 724769

Wessex Guild of Craftsmen
91 Green Lane
Clanfield
Hampshire
PO8 0LG
Tel: 01903 782529

The Makers' Guild in Wales
57 Bute Street
Cory's Building
Cardiff Bay
CF10 5AJ
Tel: 029 2049 1136

Miscellaneous

The Basketmakers' Association
King William Cottage
Yalberton Road
Paignton
Devon
TQ4 7PE
Tel: 01803 553144

British Artists' Blacksmiths' Association
111 Main Street
Ratho
Midlothian
EH28 8NW
Tel: 0131 333 1300

Calligraphy and Lettering Arts Society
54 Boileau Road
London
SW13 9BL
Tel: 020 8741 7886

British China and Porcelain Artists' Association
22 The Becks
Horncastle
Lancashire
LN9 5DF
Tel: 020 7407 7505

The Guild of British Decoupeurs
18 Pembridge Close
Charlton Kings
Cheltenham
Gloucestershire
GL52 6XY
Tel: 01604 709978

The Guild of Enamellers
10 Camellia Close
Tiverton
Devon
EX16 6TZ
Tel: 01884 255168

The Guild of Glass Engravers
35 Ossulton Way
London
N2 0JY
Tel: 020 8731 9352

Printmakers' Council
Clerkenwell Workshop
31 Clerkenwell Close
London
EC1 0AT
Tel: 020 7250 1927

The Quilling Guild
1 Clark Close
Woolavington
Bridgwater
TA7 8HE
Tel: 01279 466936

Sculptors

Royal Society of British Sculptors
108 Old Brompton Road
South Kensington
London
SW7 3RA
Tel: 020 7244 7788

Toymakers

The British Doll Artists' Association
26 Foxholes
Rudgwick
West Sussex
RH12 3DX
Tel: 01403 823596

The British Toymakers' Guild
124 Walcot Street
Bath
BA1 5BG
Tel: 01225 442440

Weavers and garment makers

Embroiderers' Guild
Apartment 41
Hampton Court Palace
East Molesey
Surrey
KT8 9AU
Tel: 020 8943 1229

The Lace Guild
53 Audnam
Stourbridge
West Midlands
DY8 4AE
Tel: 01384 390739

National Patchwork Association
PO Box 300
Hethersett
Norwich
NR9 3DB
Tel: 01603 812259

The Quilters' Guild
Room 190
Dean Clough
Halifax
West Yorkshire
HX3 5AX
Tel: 01422 347669

Association of Guilds of Weavers, Spinners and Dyers
3 Gatchell Meadow
Trull
Taunton
Somerset
TA3 7HY
Tel: 01823 325345

Publications

The Artist
Caxton House
63-65 High Street
Tenterden
TN30 6BD

Artists and Illustrators Magazine
Fitzpatrick Building
188-194 York Way
London
N7 9QR

Crafts
44a Pentonville Road
Islington
London
N1 9BY

Crafts Beautiful
Castle House
97 High Street
Colchester
CO1 1TH

The Craftsman Magazine
PO Box 61
Driffield
East Yorkshire
YO25 8JD

Needle and Hobby Crafts
Bates Business Centre
Church Road
Harold Wood
Romford
RM3 0JF

Popular Crafts
Nexus House
Azalea Drive
Swanley
BR8 8HU

Practical Craft
Traplet House
Severn Drive
Upton Upon Severn
Worcester
WR8 0JL

Writers' and Artists' Yearbook
35 Bedford Row
London
WC1R 4JH

Useful Websites

The Arts Council:	www.artscouncil.org.uk
The Crafts Council:	www.craftscouncil.org.uk
Wales Crafts Council:	www.btinternet.com/~crefft.cymru
Artists Newsletter:	www.anweb.co.uk
The Craftsman Magazine:	www.craftsman-magazine.co.uk
Small Business Service:	www.sbs.gov.uk
UK Craft Show Guide:	www.craftshows.co.uk
The Internet Craft Fair:	www.craft-fair.co.uk
Handmadecrafts:	www.handmadecrafts.co.uk

Index

RIGHT WAY
PUBLISHING POLICY

HOW WE SELECT TITLES

RIGHT WAY consider carefully every deserving manuscript. Where an author is an authority on his subject but an inexperienced writer, we provide first-class editorial help. The standards we set make sure that every **RIGHT WAY** book is practical, easy to understand, concise, informative and delightful to read. Our specialist artists are skilled at creating simple illustrations which augment the text wherever necessary.

CONSISTENT QUALITY

At every reprint our books are updated where appropriate, giving our authors the opportunity to include new information.

FAST DELIVERY

We sell **RIGHT WAY** books to the best bookshops throughout the world. It may be that your bookseller has run out of stock of a particular title. If so, he can order more from us at any time – we have a fine reputation for "same day" despatch, and we supply any order, however small (even a single copy), to any bookseller who has an account with us. We prefer you to buy from your bookseller, as this reminds him of the strong underlying public demand for **RIGHT WAY** books. However, you can order direct from us by post, by phone with a credit card, or through our web site.

FREE

If you would like an up-to-date list of all **RIGHT WAY** and **RIGHT WAY PLUS** titles currently available, please send a stamped self-addressed envelope to:

ELLIOT RIGHT WAY BOOKS, BRIGHTON ROAD, LOWER KINGSWOOD, TADWORTH, SURREY, KT20 6TD, U.K. or visit our web site at www.right-way.co.uk